UNPROCESSED

How to achieve vibrant health and your ideal weight.

By Chef AJ

with Glen Merzer

Over 100 easy, delicious, and nutrient-rich recipes!

(Gluten-free)

Foreword by Dr. Hans Diehl

Hail to the Kale Publishing.

ABOUT THE AUTHORS

CHEF AJ *has followed a plant-based diet for over 33 years. She works as a vegan/raw pastry chef in Los Angeles and as a keynote speaker and culinary instructor all across the United States. She currently resides in Los Angeles with her plant-based husband, Charles, and their two rescued mutts, Ginger (a retired therapy dog) and Sparky (a professional dog actor, model and service dog).*

GLEN MERZER *is co-author, with Howard Lyman, of* ***MAD COWBOY*** *and with Howard Lyman and Joanna Samorow-Merzer, of* ***NO MORE BULL!***

For my Pack:

Charles, Ginger, Sparky & Scooby

You are the fur beneath my feet.

TABLE OF CONTENTS

ACKNOWLEDGMENTS

Thank you to Cesar Millan, Sheila Emery, SueAnn Fincke and everyone who worked on "Dog Whisperer" for the difference you made in my life.

Thank you to Ryan Flegal for taking a chance on me and giving me my first job as a Culinary Instructor, and to all my "Kitchen Angels" who have so generously assisted me in my classes for the past 10 years – Zel Allen, Robin Blaydes, Kathy Burroughs, Diane Christofferson, Brenda Cohen, Lynn Colbert, Jennifer Ezpeleta, Wendy Gable, Ellen Greek, Miriam Isa, Stephanie Jaffe, Teresa Knotwell, Rebecca Martinez, Kenny Melcombe, Tim Ray, Bill Shalhoub, Annika Smith, Sheryl Spigel, Michelle Wolf and Andrea Zollman.

Love and Kale to you all!!!

Thank you to all of my students at the Braille Institute for teaching me how to teach, and to all of my students who have allowed me to make a difference in their lives.

Thank you to Dr. John McDougall for inspiring the two people I love the most, my husband Charles and my sister Barbara, to go plant-based, and to Mary McDougall for giving me my "big break" as a presenting chef at The McDougall Celebrity Chef Weekend.

Thank you to Dr. T. Colin Campbell for writing "The China Study" and for making my job as an educator easier.

Thank you to Dr. Neal Barnard, Dr. T. Colin Campbell, Drs. Hans & Lily Diehl, Ann Esselstyn, Dr. Caldwell B. Esselstyn, Jr., Rip Esselstyn, Dr. Joel Fuhrman, Dr. Alan Goldhamer, Dr. Jay Gordon, Louise Hay, Dr. Michael Klaper, Dr. Matthew Lederman, Dr. Doug Lisle, Howard Lyman, Dr. John McDougall, Mary McDougall, Jeff Novick, Dr. Dean Ornish, Dr. Pam Popper, Dr. Alona Pulde and John Robbins, whose works I've read and listened to over and over and use as the foundation of what I teach. It is on your shoulders I stand so that I may become tall.

Thank you to my mentor, Michael Russo, who told me to just "jump off the cliff and build my wings on the way down," and to Darren La Croix, Ed Tate and Craig Valentine, three world champions of public speaking, who taught me the six words I needed to hear to finally get this book written.

Thank you to Pastor John and Susan Jenson for helping make *Healthy Taste of L.A.* a reality.

Thank you to my co-author, Glen Merzer, for knowing that Colonel Mustard was a military officer AND a condiment.

Thank you to Dana Adelstein, Bethany Rubin, and Michelle Wolf for their eagle eyes.

And finally, thank you to my hero, Jack La Lanne, whose diet and lifestyle was an inspiration to us all, and who knew, even 80 years ago, about the evils of processed food.

Chef AJ

FOREWORD

The Good Life is killing us. Chronic diseases--diseases without a cure--have established a stronghold in our society. And the best modern medicine can do is to manage the symptoms of these modern killer diseases. But not without a cost. This year, we will spend 75% of our national $2.5 trillion health care budget on these diseases. That's $7,010 per person of our annual medical cost bill of over $9,000, which amounts to 17% of our annual income.

But there is more to the cost than money: Prescription drugs have side effects, and they can be fatal. This year alone, more than 250,000 people will have died from adverse drug reactions. This makes prescription drugs the number four cause of death in America. And most of these medications are prescribed for chronic diseases, such as heart disease, cancer, strokes, hypertension, diabetes, arthritis, heartburn, depression, and diverticular disease.

Surgical interventions may provide relief. But all too often, time erodes their benefit. In 15-30% of bypass surgeries, the grafted veins from the leg stitched into a coronary artery tree to bypass severely narrowed arteries close within 12 months of a surgery that may have cost $150,000. And some 30-45% of coronary stents designed to re-establish proper blood flow to the heart muscle may no longer be functional within the first 6 months of the intervention. Similarly, spinal fusions may have only a 50 % success rate.

Some 17% of our national earnings are now being spent on medical care. American car manufacturers are spending more money on the medical expenses of their employees than on the steel that goes into their cars. Korean manufacturers, on the other hand, spend only one-third of that amount on medical care for the workers that build their cars. This makes it difficult for American manufacturers to stay competitive in today's global economy.

Our current high-tech medical approach to these chronic Western killer diseases is no longer sustainable. We are quickly running out of options. With over 80% of all deaths from chronic diseases now being attributed to poor lifestyle choices, it is indeed becoming evident that we have reached the breaking point.

But there is hope. *The Coronary Heart Improvement Project* (**CHIP**), with more than 50,000 graduates, offers that hope. By teaching people to make simple lifestyle changes to prevent, arrest, and, in many cases, even reverse the ravages of these chronic western diseases, CHIP offers people everywhere a chance to pursue not the good life, but the "best life." And that is a life full of health, happiness, and strong social support.

And it has to do with the choices we make about our food. Chronic Western diseases relate largely to the changes in our lifestyle. And that prominently involves our food. Developing countries have to rely predominantly on unprocessed foods. They rely basically on corn and beans, potatoes and yams, wheat and rice. And that's where this book comes in. "***UNPROCESSED***" will show you the advantage of shifting from the usual processed food fare towards a more natural diet of foods-as-grown. It will help you to eat more whole foods. Nutritionally laden and inexpensive foods, such as whole grains, fresh fruits, vegetables, beans, lentils and peas. It will help you to get away from fractionated foods, from engineered and processed foods. These are the very foods that are required to carry nutrition labels, because they are usually either too high in calories, or too high in sugar, salt, fat and cholesterol and yet too low in fiber and nutritional value. Or these are the very foods that require safety labels, such as meats, chicken, turkey, eggs and fish.

As you learn how to use more of the whole foods and prepare them into delectable dishes, you will be amazed what Chef AJ, a wonderful magician of the culinary arts, has accomplished in this book. There are surprises waiting for you around every corner, every page.

Hans A. Diehl, DrHSc, MPH, CNS, FACN
Director, Lifestyle Medicine Institute
PO Box 818, Loma Linda, CA 92354
Lecturer, Dept. Medicine, Univ. of Illinois College of Medicine at Rockford
Clinical Professor of Preventive Medicine, School of Medicine, Loma Linda University
Member of Board of Directors, American College of Lifestyle Medicine (2005-2010) www.chiphealth.com

CHAPTER ONE

Can you make it in your kitchen?

My name is Abbie Jaye, but everyone calls me Chef AJ. I would like to share with you my personal story and tell you what I have learned about nutrition in a life that has often seemed to be centered around food. What you eat affects all aspects of your being, probably more than anything else you do. What you eat has a profound effect on how you feel and look. Food can cause disease, or it can prevent and reverse it. Unfortunately, I did not have this awareness for the first four decades of my life, so I would now like to share it with you in the hope that you won't have to experience the same suffering I went through and watched my loved ones endure. Both of my parents died from preventable diseases (coronary heart disease and bowel obstructions) that were brought on by diet, and I nearly destroyed my health as well. It makes me angry and it makes me determined to help others do better.

Your diet can be your undoing or your salvation. The difference is the difference between processed and unprocessed food. I'm being generous in using the term "processed food" because many processed foods scarcely deserve the label "food." When there are no nutrients in a product, why do we even think of it as food? When you eat junk, you aren't nourishing your body, just your waistline.

What do I mean by unprocessed versus processed food? Whole foods found in the produce section or the bulk section of your grocery store or farmer's market, and found there in more or less the same state that they were harvested on a farm, are *unprocessed*; packaged foods with long lists of ingredients are *processed.* Foods that have been stripped of fiber and refined are *processed.* Foods that have been concentrated and separated from the rest of the plants they come from—sugars and oils top this list—are likewise *processed.* Fruits, vegetables, pulses (beans and lentils), whole grains, nuts and seeds are *unprocessed*; *Fruit Loops* and potato chips are *processed.* Brown rice, *unprocessed*; white rice, *processed.* You get the idea.

Combining unprocessed, and only unprocessed, ingredients together by cooking or blending or mixing leaves you with a dish that remains, by my standard, unprocessed. My simple rule of thumb is this: If I can make it in my kitchen, using whole ingredients, it's unprocessed. I can cook lentils and add carrots and onions and spinach to make a soup, so that's unprocessed. I can blend fruits together to make a smoothie, so that's unprocessed. I can bake a potato or cook corn, so that's unprocessed. But I can't make a *Fruit Loop.* I can't slaughter a cow. I can't make vegetable oil, so any recipe calling for oil involves a processed ingredient. And I can't make sugar or maple syrup or agave nectar. But I do use dates as a sweetener, either whole or as date syrup or date paste, which I do make in my kitchen, so they pass my test.

All the foods that pass my test contain fiber, which fills you up with very few calories. Most of the foods that don't pass my test contain little or no fiber. The benefits of fiber to human health are gaining ever greater scientific appreciation.

Yes, there's a grey area between processed and unprocessed food. I don't often make applesauce in my kitchen, but if the only ingredient in a jar of applesauce is whole, ripe apples, it passes my test. Tofu is another food I can't easily make in my kitchen, but it's a comparatively simple food made by boiling soybeans and adding nigari or calcium sulfate, coagulating agents that separate the curd, which is then pressed. It has been made for thousands of years by the Chinese. Tofu is surely a less processed food than another high-protein form of vegan meat substitute: isolated soy protein, a highly processed ingredient that has been used as food only since 1959.

How about a whole grain bread, you might ask? Processed or unprocessed? Well, if you buy a bread whose principal ingredient is sprouted organic whole wheat berries, you're in the unprocessed end of the grey area. If you buy a bread made of white flour, you're in *Fruit Loops* territory. Trust me, you don't want to go there. To give a ranking to breads: sprouted whole grains should be preferred to whole wheat flour, and whole wheat flour should be preferred to (refined) wheat flour or, worse yet, white flour. The superior choice is eating the whole grain itself from which the bread is made.

Now, I'm a vegan and I am passionate about recommending a vegan diet—a diet containing zero animal products—to everyone. It's better for your health, better for the environment, and better for animals. But from the perspective purely of health, I'd rather see you eat a diet that is 90% vegan and 90% unprocessed (meats are by my definition inherently a processed food; most of us don't make a hot dog from scratch, starting by slaughtering the various animals whose least valuable parts wind up inside it) than a diet that is 100% vegan and only 10% unprocessed. It's very possible to eat a lousy, junky vegan diet, full of oil and sweeteners and fake meats and highly processed grains. Those foods don't require animals to die, but they won't help you live in the best of health, either. Your biological protection comes from nutrient-rich foods, not from the good karma of grateful cows.

Now, let me tell you about my long and hard road to these dietary conclusions.

CHAPTER TWO

Why should you listen to me?

I was born right after isolated soy protein in Chicago in 1960. Isolated soy protein was also created in the Windy City, which may explain my reaction to it. Both my mom and my grandmother were good cooks and I began my culinary career at the age of seven when I received an Easy Bake Oven for Hanukah. Oh, how I loved watching that light bulb magically turn batter into a real cake. I developed a serious sweet tooth early on, never realizing that my addiction to sugar could someday kill me.

The processed food industry was just beginning to become an empire in the early sixties, so while we had some of it around, mostly in the form of sweetened breakfast cereals, we also ate REAL FOOD. My mother, Lillian, cooked dinner for the family every night. Yes, we ate animal products, but there was always a salad and vegetable accompanying it, and if we wanted dessert we had to clean our plates first. Now I'm not saying this is the best way to raise your kids, but at least I did eat vegetables and I liked them. I didn't grow up like the kids you see on "Jamie Oliver's Food Revolution" who can't even identify broccoli. I always loved broccoli; unfortunately, I loved all things sweet even more.

I was overweight growing up but not obese. What's interesting is that if I could magically transport today's youths into my childhood, by today's standards I would be considered normal weight. Still, I got teased a lot; I compensated by being a straight-A student. But to a teenager, academic satisfaction pales in comparison to not being asked to your senior prom because you're too fat. Being fat hurts, inside and out.

I suffered my first major bout of depression in my early teens when I was abandoned by my father who was physically and emotionally abusive. They say that when you experience early childhood trauma like this, it affects your brain chemistry in such a way that it is even harder to deal with future traumas. When my father abandoned my family, I was sent to live in California with an aunt and uncle and two cousins. It would be almost two years until I was reunited with my mother, and while I suffered depression over the loss, in hindsight, it was the best thing that could have happened to me, for many reasons. Besides being transported to a new loving family, I now had my aunt's mother, Memé, living with us. Memé was a graduate of the Cordon Bleu and did all the cooking in the home. And when I think about what I eat today and how I teach my classes, I realize that the seeds were planted early on by this wonderful Swiss lady. Here was a woman who not only cooked real food, but made it gourmet. She could make anything taste delicious and while I lived with her, my favorite food was LEEKS!

Watching her prepare meals was better than anything you see on the Food Network today. Every meal was like eating at a five-star restaurant. She would go to the store and buy whatever was fresh and in season and create a culinary masterpiece. And she never used recipes or measured anything! (This is how I prepare food today and is why it's taken me so long to write a cookbook.) Because my aunt and her mother were European, we had salad ***after*** the meal. What a great dessert! And we always had lots of fruits and veggies, too. Even her desserts were primarily whole foods, like her *pear gallette*. And while she did use sugar, flour and butter, her pastries were not overly sweet, oily and salty like what passes for dessert today. The entire time I lived with the Harter family was a gastronomic delight. My taste buds were spoiled and I became somewhat of a snob. When my mom finally was able to come out to California, I turned my nose up one evening when she served *COOL WHIP*!

Leaving the Harter family home (and all that great food) was yet another loss and yet another adjustment. I went from a loving home where there were people around all the time to a tiny apartment with just my mom who now had to work full time. And so began my digestive decline. While my mom was an excellent cook, she now did not have time to lovingly prepare our meals from scratch like she did when she was a homemaker in Chicago. So I do understand the plight of today's working parents. More often than not, dinner was something she picked up on the way home like *Kentucky Fried Chicken* (extra crispy, of course). Gone were the days of a vegetable at every meal and salad for dessert. We were now becoming junk food junkies.

I tried to make real food, but when you're thirteen without a car or allowance, it ain't easy. I did try to cook some of our meals and surprise my mom for dinner occasionally with steamed vegetables and brown rice. And I gave my first formal dinner party at the age of fourteen. I sent out actual invitations and everything. Using the *Time Life Cookbooks*, I made Cornish Game Hens stuffed with Apple Chestnut Stuffing, Braised Hearts of Celery, and for dessert, a Bourbon Caramel Custard Cream Pie.

I was on my way to becoming a great chef -- until high school happened. Because I skipped the fourth grade, I was always younger than everyone in my class. I was also significantly heavier now that I had slipped over to the dark side (eating processed food), and a hurtful comment about my weight led me to stop eating for seven days straight. This was my first bout with anorexia nervosa, so my dreams of becoming a chef would be crushed for another twenty-five years. I would have to fight this battle with a serious eating disorder for the next eleven years.

As a junior at the University of Pennsylvania, my anorexia became so severe and my weight so low that I had to be hospitalized for several months. I was scared to be all alone in a hospital in Philadelphia, so I was transferred to one in Los Angeles. I still remember the embarrassment and shame I felt when my sister-in-law, Lauren, picked me up to take me home.

They did not have any really state-of-the-art treatments for anorexia in the late seventies. It went like more or less like this: Either you eat or we stick a tube down your throat and feed you. So I had the choice of either eating crappy hospital food or being tubed. I chose the former. (Did you ever wonder why people who could benefit from good nutrition the most, like hospital patients and school children, are served the worst food?) Oh, and they had someone watching you at all times so you couldn't purge and they wouldn't let you exercise. I ate what they served me to get the weight back on so I could get the hell out of the hospital. The nurse would tell me how I permanently damaged myself with this disease and how I really screwed up my hypothalamus and liver and other organs. I didn't care; I just wanted to go home, and would do anything to get out of the hospital.

While I was hospitalized for anorexia, I developed some serious medical complications. Unlike many Americans who worry unnecessarily about this condition, I actually ***was*** protein deficient. But, as Dr. Matthew Lederman will tell you, you can't be protein deficient without being calorie deficient and I was literally starving myself to death. My hair and fingernails fell out; I stopped getting menstrual periods. An endoscopy showed that the vomiting I did after bingeing burned my esophagus. I was very sick and very difficult. I will always regret what I put my family through.

Unfortunately, when I did start eating again, I didn't choose a plant-based, nutrient-rich, whole-food diet. I chose crap. All the treats I had been denying myself for years, I now ate with abandon. This is when my sugar addiction kicked into full gear. I was on a first name basis with every salesperson at *Weby's* and *Skandia* bakeries, and I knew what was inside every piece of *See's Candy*. My nightly dinner became a hot fudge sundae from *Baskin Robbins* with *Baseball Nut* or *Pralines and Cream* ice cream. Double fudge, extra nuts.

That was bad enough, but on top of it I also completely stopped eating fruits and vegetables. I was required to gain only twenty pounds to no longer be underweight and get out of the hospital, but I literally could not stop eating what Dr. David Kessler calls "hyper palatable food," comprised of the perfect combination of sugar, fat, and salt. My new way of eating really put the anorexia behind me: I ended up gaining sixty pounds! That was thirty pounds more than I weighed before I started losing weight on my journey to anorexia.

So now, for the first time in my life, I was officially obese. Due to my messed-up GI system, I could no longer force myself to vomit, so to lose weight I began to exercise—and I became addicted to that, too. I also purposely took up smoking cigarettes (which I thankfully was able to stop just a few years later due to a broken rib). Anyway, addiction is addiction is addiction. Those of us whose brain chemistry allows us to become quickly and easily addicted to one substance can also become easily addicted to another. I never realized I had an addiction problem because my doctor had said that sugar is not addictive! But of course it is, and that's why food manufacturers—a fitting name, *food manufacturers*—put it in everything from infant formula to geriatric formula.

Within months of getting out of the hospital, I had become really ill. I developed adult onset asthma and needed to take hundreds of dollars' worth of medication every month. I was constantly injecting myself with epinephrine. I was then in a serious accident in which my spine was crushed. I was temporarily paralyzed and was in a body cast for a year. The only positive side of that experience: You can't binge in a body cast, it's too tight. All of these illnesses and injuries led to my using up all of the benefits on my mom's health insurance and I was dropped. Fair to say, I had hit rock bottom.

Unable to live like this anymore, I turned to God. Maybe not the most original move for an addict, but it worked for me. While I did not join a twelve-step program (is there even a Sweet Tooth Anonymous?), I began a spiritual practice that involved yoga and meditation. I also read a book that would forever change my life, *You Can Heal Your Life* by Louise Hay. For probably the first time in my life, I hit my knees and prayed to God. I remember saying, "Please, just allow me to eat like a normal person and I will accept any weight *You* want me to be so long as I can easily maintain it without fasting, bingeing or over-exercising." In retrospect, since it appears that *Someone* was listening, the wording of my prayer may have been a strategic mistake. I should have asked to be thinner.

In 1987, after being a vegetarian for ten years, I became involved with an animal rights organization and became vegan. From the beginning, I never understood how we decided that some species are food and others are pets. And once it was explained to me how dairy cows suffer a fate worse than beef cattle and how cruelly chickens are treated, going vegan was a no-brainer. It was easy to do and I've never looked back. Even though I hadn't been drinking milk or eating cheese or eggs, I had been eating desserts made from these unhealthy ingredients, so once I could no longer eat them my weight stabilized and my asthma disappeared. Unfortunately, I still found a way to indulge my sweet tooth by making sugary vegan desserts, so a skinny herbivore I would not be.

In my late twenties and thirties, a generally happier time, I began acting and performing comedy. I realized a life-long dream by appearing on several television shows, including "The Tonight Show" with Johnny Carson, on which I performed my signature act of playing two flutes through my nose while standing on my head and blowing bubble gum out of my mouth. I also met my husband, Charles. We got married in 1995, the same year I graduated college.

We took a Mexican cruise on our honeymoon, and being the accident-prone Aries I am, something told me to buy the insurance. And boy, am I glad I did. I developed a life-threatening lung and liver infection in Ensenada, and my hospital bill for just three days was over twenty thousand dollars. I learned again, as if I ever needed reminding, that the only thing I hate more than going to a funeral is being a patient in a hospital.

After I got married, I started having some knee pain from doing step aerobics. During the resulting inactivity, I gained some weight. This is when Phen Fen was at its height of popularity. My doctor prescribed it for me and I lost tons of weight easily and effortlessly and I felt great mentally, too. I had never felt better! Now, with the addition to my diet of Phen Fen, I was still eating vegan crap, but my brain was tricked into eating less of it. And then the FDA pulled the drug off the market due to serious heart and lung side effects. I had an echocardiogram to see if there was any valve damage, and I was lucky; there wasn't.

But it wouldn't be long before my horrible diet would catch up with me.

When I was 39, I finally got pregnant. We had tried for so many years and I was so excited! In January of 2000, I began bleeding. My OB/GYN wanted to do an amniocentesis. I knew there were risks involved with this procedure and tried to decline. He said that he needed to know what we were up against come delivery and convinced me to have it.

The funny thing about the procedure was that my husband fainted. It would be many years until I would find anything funny again. The results came back that the baby, a girl whom we had named Rachel and seen wave to us during the last ultrasound, had Down's Syndrome. I was devastated but I still wanted to have the baby. I was told there was more to know and I would need to see a high-risk neonatologist immediately because in three days, the state of California would deem the baby a live birth and I would not be able to do anything about it.

Seeing the high-risk neonatologist was one of the worst days of my life. The doctor said that the baby had no tricuspid valve and had a hole in each of the four chambers of her heart. If she did make it to term, she would need to have immediate and frequent open heart surgeries. We had twenty-four hours to decide if we wanted to terminate the pregnancy. Charles and I decided we did not want her to suffer, so I signed the consent form allowing the doctor to terminate the "flawed pregnancy."

I wouldn't wish the loss of a child on my worst enemy. What made it worse is when people would say things like, "Well, it wasn't a real baby." Let me tell you, the minute you find out you're pregnant, IT IS REAL and you are already in love with this person you've never even met. I fell into another deep depression. I didn't even want to live anymore. But I didn't have time to grieve for long before I got call from an ICU nurse in Illinois that my father was very ill.

Even though I had seen my father only twice from the age of eleven to the age of forty, he had made me the executor of his will. The laws are different in Illinois, so I had to fly back there, still bleeding from my own operation, to manage the end of his life. He had suffered from coronary artery disease even before I was born. He had his first heart attack before the age of fifty. While he was not overweight like my mother, he did have high blood pressure and high cholesterol and ate the Standard American Diet, with a Jewish twist. He loved his daily slice of kosher salami like a fat boy loves cake. In the end, it killed him. He was already on all the medications you can be on for heart disease and nothing helped. He had overcome prostate cancer but couldn't take the daily chest pains. So he opted for open heart surgery, which failed. I watched him languish in the ICU the last nineteen long days of his life, as first he was put on a ventilator, then a feeding tube, then a tracheotomy tube. His hands were tied down so he would not pull the tubes out. He could not speak, but you could see the terror in his eyes as he languished for almost three weeks in a helpless state. And for what? For his love of kosher salami.

Kosher salami, for those of you taking notes, differs from regular salami in that one kills you and the other is blessed by a rabbi before it kills you.

After I lost my baby and then my dad, my beloved dog, Scooby died, and then my mom developed severe dementia and congestive heart failure, all caused by her diet. I had to become her primary caregiver for the last four years of her life, watching her deteriorate slowly and insidiously.

During that terrible period in my life, I suffered three more miscarriages and required multiple operations to correct problems caused by a piece of fetal thoracic bone lodged in my uterus from the death of the first baby. When I left my home, I began having panic attacks for which I couldn't receive medication during the periods when I was pregnant.

After my last operation, the surgeon said that he was sorry, but I would not be able to have children. Like a computer that crashes, my brain completely short-circuited. I couldn't work, so I quit my job and we wound up losing our home. I developed panic disorder with agoraphobia so severe that until Sparky was trained to be my service dog, I didn't leave my house for almost a year.

All the emotional trauma I suffered took a toll on my diet and my health. My sugar addiction went through the roof. I was so depressed I didn't want to eat, and if I did, it had to be something sweet. They say "to grieve well is to live well," and I was doing a pretty poor job at both. One of the teachers at *Dick and Jane Cook Vegetarian*, the culinary school where I was teaching, told me that I was eating all this sugar to compensate for the lack of sweetness in my life. I had a few choice words to say to him, but I sure wish I could find him now and apologize and tell him he was right.

Here's what my diet consisted of for years. For breakfast, I would have a thirty-two ounce *Coke Slurpee* with eight pumps of vanilla syrup. For lunch, I drank a forty-eight ounce *Big Gulp Dr.*

Pepper. During this time, I was working sixty hours a week as an Activity Director at a retirement home. By four p.m., I couldn't keep my eyes open so I would have some type of vegan pastry. Thankfully, Javier, the chef at the facility, would make me some steamed broccoli with marinara sauce every night before I went home, my only real sustenance. I would go home, exhausted, feeling really bad about myself, knowing that practically nothing I ate that day remotely resembled food. Finally, I got a bright red wake-up call.

On January 1, 2003, I woke up and tried to have a bowel movement. Instead, the entire toilet bowl was filled with bright red blood. I was really terrified. My grandmother had died of colon cancer, my mom and my other grandmother of a bowel obstruction, and one of my uncles had recently had eighty percent of his colon removed. I was worried that something was seriously wrong. I went to my HMO and told them I wanted a colonoscopy and they refused, stating it would have to be a first-degree relative who had the cancer to warrant a colonoscopy. They told me it was probably just hemorrhoids. Hemorrhoids? I had a hemorroidectomy in 1985 and, at their worst, they NEVER bled profusely like this. After jumping through all the crazy hoops of the HMO, I finally received a sigmoidoscopy which, sure enough, showed that I had several large, bleeding adenomatous polyps in my sigmoid colon. These are the kind that Dr. Oz had and, if not removed, usually become cancer. They called them "pre-cancerous" and that was a big enough of a wake-up call for me. My colon was so filthy and in such bad shape from forty-three years of abuse that the doctors said they could not remove the polyps because they couldn't get "a clean shot." Even with that awful prep they have you do before a procedure, they were able to photograph the polyps but not remove them without risking serious infection. They told me I would have to come back for further intervention. Well, if there is one benefit of my panic disorder, it's that I am deathly afraid of taking most medications and having most procedures. Above all, I have an unnatural and exaggerated fear of surgery and general anesthesia. When I had an endoscopy, I was so afraid of even the "light sedation" that they did the whole thing with me completely awake.

So, instead of drugs or surgery, I took another path that would change the course of my life forever. I used diet. I figured that if my food choices could either cause or at least greatly contribute to this disease, would it not also be possible for better food choices to reverse it? So I opted to go the "drastic route"—as healthy dietary changes are generally labeled—and on Sunday, July 6, 2003, I had my last *Coke Slurpee* and checked into the Optimum Health Institute (OHI) in San Diego, California. While it may be true that I had a genetic predisposition for developing colon cancer, genetics, in fact, only account for 1-3% of whether a cancer gene expresses and you actually get the disease. Genetics only load the gun - **DIET AND LIFESTYLE PULL THE TRIGGER!**

Going to OHI was one of the best decisions I ever made in my life. There I met interesting people from all over the world, including many celebrities who were there just to lose weight, and pro football players there to make weight before the season started. But there were also many people who had very serious illnesses such as brain cancer, lupus and even AIDS. OHI is not a medical facility and we were not allowed to even talk about our diseases or, as they liked to call it, our "health opportunities." But every Friday, graduates of the program would come back and give testimonials of their healing and I was deeply moved. They had diseases far more serious than mine, so I figured getting rid of these polyps would be a piece of cake.

Every day from morning until night I took classes that dealt with healing on three levels -- body, mind, and spirit. But the most important education I got was at mealtime. The diet they prescribed was not only plant-based, it was organic and 100% raw. And, unlike the diet of many raw foodists today, with tons of highly processed, low-nutrient foods like agave, coconut oil and olive oil, the OHI diet was free of what I have come to call "The Evil Trinity" (sugar, oil and salt). Instead, it was based on fruits, vegetables, sprouts and seeds. For breakfast, we had watermelon. For lunch, a salad with vegetables, sprouts and seed cheese made of sesame and sunflower seeds. Dinner was the same and there was no dressing. AND NO DESSERT!

On three of the days we did a juice fast and I thought I was gonna die. I would call my husband and sister every night and beg them to get me out of there. Like every addict who eventually comes clean, I was going through severe withdrawal and detox. In addition to the food, every day we drank something called *Rejuvelac*, plenty of water, and freshly grown wheatgrass. Colonics were optional but we also were instructed on how to give ourselves daily enemas and wheatgrass implants. For a woman who had stood on her head on "The Tonight Show," this wasn't hard.

I have always had a "when in Rome" attitude. So I complied with the program one hundred percent. At OHI, the abiding philosophy is that disease occurs when the body is in an acidic state and that pretty much everything consumed on the Standard American Diet (meat, cheese, dairy, eggs, sugar, flour, caffeine, alcohol, oil, salt, processed food) serves to make us acidic. We were taught that we need to alkalize our bodies, not by drinking some expensive water, but by eating fruits and vegetables in their raw state.

While abstaining from animal products was not a problem for me, I had spent four decades eating from my own set of the four basic food groups: sugar, flour, oil and caffeine. I remembered that at my fortieth birthday party at the Excalibur Hotel in Las Vegas, my family had roasted me. Charles had said, "My wife is the only vegetarian who never eats fruits or vegetables. The only greens she gets are in a bag of Skittles." He was right.

Today, while I empathize with my students who tell me it's hard for them to give up their animal products, trust me, it was just as hard, initially, for me to go from my vegan junk food diet to the diet I enjoy and advocate today.

When I got home from OHI, I felt better physically and emotionally than I had in my entire life. I was slimmer and looked healthier and younger. My skin was clear and my eyes sparkled. When I arrived home, I was so calm and serene that my own dogs didn't recognize me. They looked confused and kept sniffing me as if they didn't know who I was. At home, I continued with the diet and the visualization techniques I had learned at OHI. For everyone it's different, but because my husband loves the game Pac Man, every day I would visualize the little yellow man going through my colon and eating up the polyps as the video game theme song played in my head. ☺

Six months later, I went for a follow-up sigmoidoscopy and my colon was completely clear! The doctors said it was remarkably clean this time, pink and vascular like a newborn's, and they kept poking and prodding me looking for the polyps to remove. They said they had photographs indicating their size and exact location and now they were completely gone. They even accused me of going outside the HMO to get them removed! I told them that all I did was change my diet and they told me, "That's impossible!" Afterwards, one of the doctors, who happened to be from India, quietly whispered in my ear, "I believe you."

Well, I believed me, too. I knew that a series of emotional traumas, one after the other, had aggravated my tendency to turn to sweet, fatty, and salty foods for comfort, and that sweets in particular had become an addiction. I knew that my addiction had eventually threatened my health and my life. And I knew that eating whole, raw, unprocessed food had done what my doctors believed was impossible, restoring my health and saving me from their interventions.

I was elated by this news but I knew that if I was going to keep eating this way, it would have to be more than sprouts and wheatgrass. It would have to taste delicious! So I took a leave of absence from my job and went to culinary school. Even though it was a raw and vegan culinary school (the Living Light Culinary Arts

Institute), the food was much richer than the food they taught us to eat at OHI. Every recipe had salt and either coconut oil or olive oil, and agave had just hit the scene.

Still, I was consuming a ton of fruits and veggies now on a daily basis so I was still way ahead of where I had previously been nutritionally. One of the most valuable things I learned was how to make a green smoothie, which I have been enjoying every day for breakfast for the last seven years. There is nothing like starting your day with a half a pound of spinach or kale!

Two years after my polyp diagnosis, I finally enrolled with a PPO. I immediately went back to my regular doctor and told him about my situation. He did a colonoscopy and he said that all was clear and that I did not have to come back for another ten years.

I started eating cooked vegan food again while making sure I also ate plenty of raw fruits and vegetables. I had done research and concluded that while a strict raw food diet proved invaluable to me by reversing my disease, one can also stay healthy and thrive while eating some cooked foods. The most important lesson that I had learned at OHI was to completely stop eating white sugar, white flour and almost all processed food. I've never wavered on that conclusion and I've never regretted it.

My dietary objective became, quite simply, to eat **a whole food, plant-based diet with no added sugar, oil, or salt and absolutely no processed food**. I eat as many fruits and vegetables as I desire, with the addition of beans, lentils, whole grains and a small amount of raw nuts and seeds.

I had heard about not using oil over twenty years earlier when I read *The McDougall Plan* by Dr. John McDougall. He often says, "The fat you eat is the fat you wear." But while I knew that oil was really fattening, I really had no idea it was actually harmful until reading *Prevent and Reverse Heart Disease* by Dr. Caldwell B. Esselstyn, Jr. He talks about the Brachial Artery Tourniquet Test and how even a single meal with oil can injure the epithelial tissue of your arteries. So I learned that not only is oil not the heart healthy food we were led to believe, it actually is an injurious food that helps promote diabetes and heart disease.

Clearly, the oil had to go. What was really interesting is that when we gave up oil, my husband, who was never overweight, lost an additional twenty-five pounds without making any other dietary changes. And seven months after we cut oil out of our diet, an unsightly tumor on his spine shrank to the size of a nickel! I can only wonder what eliminating oil would do for cancer.

Salt was really not at all difficult for me to give up. Sure, I would put salt in a recipe that called for it, but I never added it to my food. My grandparents and parents already had advanced heart disease by the time I was born, so I grew up not eating salt. I remember when I was seven years old someone gave me a pretzel rod with the coarse salt on the outside. I took one bite and almost vomited. It tasted like when an ocean wave hits you and you swallow all that salt water. If you grow up without eating salt, you really do not crave it.

There are many culinary tricks I will teach you later on that will help you curb your salt tooth, but in the meantime, if you still MUST consume it, do as Dr. McDougall says and only sprinkle it on the surface of your food (what we chefs call "the finish"). Never cook with salt as you will use way too much and the flavor will dissipate in the cooking. Use only enough salt to make these otherwise healthy foods taste delicious. I tell my students to buy the most expensive sea salt they can buy so they will use it gingerly because it is so costly.

But what about sugar? I had completely given up white sugar on July 6, 2003, and was now consuming only agave and maple syrup. But now I had learned that they were nutritionally almost indistinguishable from white sugar. As with oil, the only good sugar is none. While maple syrup and molasses may have minute amounts of minerals, we don't eat processed sweeteners to satisfy out daily minimum requirement for minerals. We don't sprinkle processed sweeteners on our broccoli. We tend to use them to sweeten foods that are otherwise unhealthy and nutritionally bereft, products whose other ingredients are likely to be flour and oil. So if you ask me today what the healthiest sweetener is, I will tell you NONE. And if you ask me what the healthiest dessert is, I will tell you FRUIT.

I remember hearing Dr. T. Colin Campbell joke about these three ingredients, saying, "Sugar, oil, flour – that's a doughnut!" But I had been working as a pastry chef and these were the three ingredients I was using the most! I thought I was doing a good thing using agave and maple syrup instead of sugar, using spelt or barley flour instead of white flour, and using coconut oil instead of butter. Desserts were my life, both making them and eating them. How could this be, that the three ingredients they were primarily composed of were, perhaps after animal products, the WORST things to consume? I never had thought about how processing a food makes it more calorie rich and nutrient poor.

I was trying to accompany a friend, who had a cancer diagnosis, on a three-week, salt-free, oil-free, sugar-free diet. And the sugar part was the part that was tripping me up. The seeker in me really wanted to figure out why I could not go one day, let alone three weeks, without a sweet treat. When I would open the freezer and start crying, it wasn't the kind of crying you do when you, say, stub your toe. It was the kind of crying you hear from a frightened little kid in a department store who can't find his or her mommy. The kind of crying you hear on the National Geographic Channel when a young cub is taken from its mother. It was crying from the depths of my soul. The kind of crying I did when Rachel died. It was almost eight years since she died and I realized I had never fully grieved for her or let go of the pain of the decision to terminate the pregnancy. It was so much easier to medicate myself with food, my drug of choice being dessert. I could get through the day without "my drug" by keeping constantly busy, always in motion. Once I was home, in the quiet of the night, I simply could not stand being alone with my thoughts and my feelings. It was so much easier to eat a few homemade vegan chocolate cherry cookies with crystallized ginger and just numb out. So now I kept saying to myself, "It's only grief, it's not going to kill me" and "This too shall pass." And it did.

The three weeks passed and, after being off processed sugar, my palate readjusted. Now, for the first time in my life, I could taste the sweetness in fruit and I loved it. A frozen grape tasted like sorbet from a fine restaurant. I fell in love with Gala apples, pluots and Mexican papaya. Sometimes when I eat fruit now it tastes almost too sweet to me. Whether it's sugar or salt, your palate *will* readjust and you will start appreciating the sweetness and saltiness inherent in all whole plant food. But this can't happen if you constantly stimulate your taste buds with sugar and salt. Remember, the ONLY thing that works for addiction is complete and total abstinence. Moderation does not work for an addict.

CHAPTER THREE
Do you really want to do this?

I am hoping that by reading my life's story, you may have had your interest piqued about the many benefits of eating a whole food, plant-based diet, free of sugar, oil and salt. Some of you may already be convinced that this is the best way to eat but are convinced that *you* could never eat this way.

Well, first let me say that I didn't start eating this way overnight. It took me almost fifty years to find the diet that worked best for me, so I don't expect you to do it all at once, either. And unless you currently have a serious disease like cancer, heart disease or diabetes, I wouldn't encourage you to do it all at once, unless you are one of these "all or none" personality types and you are sure you can handle it. My best advice to you is to just do ***something***. Just because you can't do ***everything*** doesn't mean you shouldn't do ***anything***. Optimum health exists on a continuum and even small, incremental changes made consistently over time can still be of great benefit. Take my student Matthew. He was not ready to do everything all at once. But he agreed to substitute his standard American breakfast everyday for a green smoothie, and in a year, he lost thirty pounds and went to his forty-fifth high school reunion at his senior class weight. You have to decide what your personal health goals are and how quickly you want to reach them.

Many of you have been eating poorly for a very long time. The longer you have been eating this way, the harder it may be for you to change and the more difficult the period of detox and withdrawal may be. But that by no means is a reason not to do it. The first step in any journey is making the conscious decision to embark upon it. Despite all the convincing evidence on how you can lose weight and quickly and easily reverse the common diseases of affluence and lifestyle, maybe you just aren't ready. I have found that often the sicker the person is, the more willing he or she is to make major changes immediately. If you aren't ready, that's okay. If you want to wait until your health deteriorates further, that's always an option. Just keep this book on hand for when you are sick enough or fat enough and are ready to change. Or give it to someone else whose life may be saved by this information.

If you truly think you are ready to start your journey towards optimum health and your ideal weight, the first step is to make a commitment that you will do this for at least thirty days. As my mentor Michael Russo says, you really only have two choices in life. You either commit to doing something or commit to your excuses about why you can't do something. If you're a Star Wars fan, you know what Yoda would tell you: "Do or do not do. There is no try." If you do this program, as prescribed, for thirty days and you do not see an improvement in your health, let me know because you'll be the first. What you should be asking of yourself is progress, not perfection. Do you know anyone who eats perfectly all the time? I do not. I am not perfect and I am not asking you to be perfect. All I am asking from you is a serious commitment to a new approach to eating for a period of thirty days. Do you think you're up for the challenge?

I can hear the little voice in your head screaming "Yeah, but…." If you are what I lovingly call a YABBUT, let's go over some of the common fears people have when embracing a new, healthier lifestyle. I call these myths because I am able to debunk each of them. But before I do, please keep in mind that if this is something that you truly want to do, there are no excuses. The fact that you are even reading this book tells me that you are the kind of person who can see the possibility of something wonderful for your life, for your health, and for the health of your family. I'm guessing you've already done many difficult things in your life and have succeeded at them, so why should this be any different?

I studied acting with a brilliant teacher named Joan Darling. She won an Emmy for directing the hilarious episode of "The Mary Tyler Moore Show" called "Chuckles Bites the Dust." In our acting class, we had everyone from a young child who had never acted to Academy Award nominated actors. Many would ask Joan if they had what it took to succeed as a professional working actor, using the phrase, "Have I got it?" Joan's answer was always the same: "How bad do you want it?" I am giving you all the tools you need to succeed and to have boundless energy and amazing health. You only have to ask yourself one question and answer it honestly: How bad do YOU want it?

YABBUT # 1 – It's too expensive to eat this way.

It is absolutely true that fast food and processed food are cheap, fast and easy. But if you continue to eat it, please also know that recovering from heart bypass surgery or foot amputation from diabetes is expensive, difficult and slow. It's interesting how many people who come into my class and say they can't afford to eat this way are carrying the largest size designer coffee from Starbucks. And you know this isn't the first time they went there. They are paying at least $3 a day for their favorite drugs, caffeine and sugar. And many of them are also sporting a Kate Spade handbag. It really is a matter of priorities. If your health was a priority, we wouldn't even be having this conversation. You're an adult and you have every right to choose to eat whatever you want. (But, by the way, I don't believe you should have the right to feed this crap to your children.)

You are right; it can be more expensive, especially in the beginning, to eat this way. But it doesn't have to be. There are tons of FREE resources on www.drmcdougall.com that can prove to you how this way of eating can even be less expensive. Or get Jeff Novick's DVD *Fast Food.* Or let prolific cookbook author Robin Robertson show you how affordable it can be in her new book, *Vegan on the Cheap*.

Many people say they cannot afford organic. And while I certainly want to support organic farming practices whenever possible, it's like Dr. Matthew Lederman says: "People are not fat and sick because they choose to eat conventionally produced produce over organic. It's because they are not eating fruits and vegetables." I have seen huge bunches of organic kale at Whole Foods on sale for ninety-nine cents a bunch. When you see this, stock up. If you can't afford ninety-nine cents, I have seen beautiful kale at ethnic markets for as low as forty-nine cents a bunch. Just be sure you wash it well. Even discount stores such as Wal-Mart and the 99 Cents Only store have organics now. You can also buy frozen fruits and veggies which are often more nutritious than fresh. Fresh produce is often picked and then sits on a truck for a week until it gets to you. Fruits and vegetables are picked at their peak and flash frozen, so very few nutrients are lost. You can often find these items on sale at your grocery store, so stock up. Just be sure that the fruit you buy has no sugar added. Almost every city has a farmer's market now, and that's a great place to buy fresh, affordable produce.

A large part of your diet should be comprised of starchy vegetables, whole grains, and legumes. None of these items is expensive to begin with, but if you buy them in the bulk section they are even cheaper. Potatoes, beans and rice are some of the least expensive foods you can buy.

You know that when you really want something in life, you somehow have the money for it. And if you really want your food to be cheap, grow it yourself. But if you aren't ready to eat this way yet, that's okay. More kale for me!

YABBUT # 2 - I don't have the time to prepare healthy food.

This one really cracks me up because many people cannot even sit through my classes without constantly typing on their Crackberry. You can see the angst in their eyes if their beloved handheld device makes a sound and I ask them to please shut it off. It's like they will die if they can't constantly attend to its needs. I can't tell you how many times I will go on Facebook or Twitter after my classes and read posts by people that were made ***during*** the class. Just like you can't text and drive, you can't possibly learn what I have to teach you at the same time you are addicted to your technology of choice. Some of you are being raised on it so you know no other way. For many of you, it is an addiction, just like white cupcakes with buttercream frosting and rainbow sprinkles used to be for me. By staying constantly electronically connected, you don't have to ever be alone and your time-saving device somehow manages to leave you with no time for anything. How much time do you spend on Facebook, or tweeting, blogging, texting, or checking your e-mail? How much time do you spend surfing the net, playing video games, or watching TV? The truth is, we all have enough time for things we truly value. If you make your health, and the health of your children, truly your number one priority, time ceases to be an issue.

Eating the whole plant foods that your body was designed to eat will give you so much more energy that you will probably need to sleep less and as a result will actually have ***more*** time. And in the recipe section you will learn ways to prepare this food that take less time than conventional cooking methods. Take soup preparation for example. A standard soup recipe almost always asks you to sauté an onion in 2-4 tablespoons of olive oil. Well, that step takes time. In my soup recipes you throw everything in, often without even cutting it up! And as far as taste is concerned, I once prepared two otherwise identical batches of soup, one with and the other without the oil. No one could even tell the difference. So why add an extra five hundred calories when you don't need it? By not using oil, you will save time, money and calories.

Another way to save time is to use the cook-once, eat-twice method. When you are preparing food, make sure you have enough for leftovers and snacks. If you're going to bake one potato, you might as well bake four. They are great the next day, even cold. It's also important to always have healthy food on hand so you won't eat crap just because you're hungry. Fail to plan and plan to fail. While canned beans are more expensive than bulk, you can buy a wide variety of salt-free canned beans at Whole Foods for under a buck a can. If you are truly worried about the BPAs in the metal, buy Eden beans which are BPA-free. See if you can enroll a friend or neighbor to eat this way and take turns making meals. My friend, Michelle, got most of her colleagues to take my class and they were inspired to eat this way. Now each one of them makes lunch only one day a week for the whole group. They not only save time but get to share recipes and have great variety. While preparing healthy food may never be as fast as going through the drive-through window (and how long are some people willing to sit in cars in lines for the drive-through window?), it can be as fast as cooking in an unhealthy manner or eating processed food. In one of my You Tube videos I make decadent Black Bean Brownies from scratch in less time than it would take for you to open up a brownie mix.

When you go to the store to buy produce, bring your green bags with you. This not only helps the environment by not wasting another plastic bag, but it saves time because you can then put the items directly into your refrigerator. Make a green smoothie for breakfast and drink it in the car on the way to work. You can even place the ingredients in the blender the night before so all you have to do in the morning is push the button. At Trader Joe's and some other stores you can buy lots of reasonably priced organic produce, much of which is already washed and cut up. If you don't have time to cut up lettuce and vegetables, buy them in the bags. They have several varieties of lettuces as well as the darker leafy greens like spinach and collards, pre-washed and cut up. You can also find shredded cabbage in purple and white, carrots, broccoli slaw, and pre-cut onions. You can now even find peeled garlic and prewashed leeks. True, it is a bit more costly this way, so if you need to save money, see YABBUT #1.

With the exception of my lasagna recipe, which is more of a celebration recipe, most of my recipes can be prepared in minutes and take less than thirty minutes to cook. When I was teaching healthy cooking to the blind at the Braille Institute, they had ninety minutes to prepare a five-course meal. The blind had no trouble doing it. Almost every recipe in this book was prepared by one of my blind students. Even my husband can prepare them!

YABBUT # 3 – But I can't live without my (fill in the blank).

Well, if that's truly the case, then you, my friend, are addicted. If I told you I could guarantee you would never have diabetes, cancer, a heart attack or stroke, but you could never have okra again, do you think you could cope? I would venture to say yes, because you probably are not addicted to okra. Attendance is light at the Okra Anonymous meetings. But if I tell you to give up cheese or meat or sugar or chocolate, you say it can't be done! (I will never ask you to give up chocolate, just the dairy and sugar that often accompany it.)

I think part of the problem is that people don't like the word "addict." It conjures up the image of some derelict in a dark alley shooting up heroin. The definition of addiction is a compulsive physiological and/or psychological need for a habit-forming substance. (And any substance can be habit forming.) If you are not addicted to these foods, then why is it so hard, if not impossible, for you to give them up? Why does just the thought of giving them up make you sad or anxious?

Remember this: Processed food was designed to be addictive. How do you like being manipulated on a biochemical level? Instead of lusting after processed food, you might consider resenting its manufacturers for attempting to control your body. When you get angry enough about it, you may stop buying it all together. Keep in mind that some processed food companies are owned by tobacco companies, true champions of addiction, and another industry you might not want to support.

Imagine that there's a party and I'm going to serve four different bowls of popcorn. The first bowl is air-popped popcorn with nothing on it. The second bowl is popped in oil but is unsalted. The third bowl is popped in oil and has just the right amount of salt on it. And the fourth bowl is Kettle Corn, popped in oil with the perfect combination of both sugar and salt on it. Most people would choose the third or the fourth bowl, and I bet you dollars to doughnuts that if I were catering a party I would have to refill the fourth bowl the most often.

Sugar, fat and salt work together to make food damn near irresistible, which is why it makes its appearance in just about everything you love. While *McDonald's* French fries taste primarily of salt and fat, they also have sugar in them. The same is true of most potato chips. Even things that taste primarily sweet, like a *Cinnabon*, have salt added. I think you will be hard-pressed to find any processed food (or restaurant food for that matter) that isn't comprised of a large quantity of sugar, fat, and salt. When the old TV commercial for a popular potato chip said, "Betcha can't eat just one," they were right. They knew all about how your brain chemistry works and they designed their product to exploit what they knew.

We all have dopamine receptors in our brains. Dopamine is a neurotransmitter that is released in our brain whenever we have a pleasurable experience. This could be having sex, taking illicit drugs, or even eating highly caloric food like a *Big Mac*, fries and a *Coke* (a very popular combination of sugar, fat and salt).

Unfortunately, the more highly caloric the food, the more dopamine is released, so we continue to choose these unhealthy foods to get more of a dopamine hit. This is especially true if we are feeling bad, or sad, or under stress. We become habituated to this amount of dopamine and have to keep eating more and more processed food laden with sugar, fat and salt to get the same amount of pleasure. And the earlier in a child's life that you start feeding him this crap, the more difficult it is to break this cycle. It's not unlike a heroin addict who spends his whole life chasing that first high he experienced when he tried the drug. He now requires more and more of the drug, not even to feel good anymore, instead just so he won't feel bad.

You can't just cut down on a substance you are addicted to and expect to regain your health. You need to quit. Just like people who quit smoking or stop drinking coffee, you will feel bad initially. But remember, the only way out is through. There is a light at the end of the tunnel, because eventually you will feel so amazing and look so great that you won't be able even to imagine going back to the dark side. And if you can't do this, that's okay too. I understand that change is difficult. And some people would rather die than change.

YABBUT # 4 - But my friends and family won't support me in this.

I'm not going lie to you; it is easier with the support of your loved ones. But it can be done without it. My sister (who went from a size 14 to a size 4 in seven months from eating this way and lowered her cholesterol and triglycerides to a healthy level) did this completely on her own. Her husband did not want to eat this way with her. While it would be great if you had the support of all your friends and family, that just may not be a reality for you. In fact, they may not only *not* support you, they may try to sabotage your efforts, especially if they are unhealthy themselves. This is sad, but true. Perhaps they are afraid that if you get well, you will leave them. Or that you will start making them wrong for the way they eat. Or that you will become slim and healthy while they stay fat and sick. Or it could be that if you start acknowledging your addiction, they may be forced to acknowledge theirs. They may feel very confronted by your attempts to lead a healthier life. So my advice to you is to leave them alone. You can't change them anyway, so just work on yourself. In time, when they see the change in you, they may become interested and ask you what you're doing.

Pamela, a woman in her fifties, was the first winner of our 30 Day Challenge. She became a size 6 and posted photos of herself on Facebook in a bikini and everyone wanted to know what she was doing. They weren't even interested in the fact that she lowered her cholesterol to the point where she no longer needed medication, they just cared that she looked hot!

It's interesting how when you are eating crap, no one cares or comments (except for me!). But the minute you start eating healthfully, all of a sudden, everyone is a nutritionist. And they will say the most absurd and unfounded things.

You might want to go to www.chipusa.org and see if there is a CHIP program near you. If you can, find a buddy, even an on-line one. You can join the McDougall Boards for free and also find many *Yahoo*, *Google* or *Meetup* groups dedicated to healthy eating.

Try explaining to your family how important this is to you. That you want to eat this way so that you will be around a long time to take care of them and be there for them. Unfortunately, most people don't realize the consequences of their lifelong food choices until it's almost too late. Try to make it fun for them. Research shows that kids will eat what they prepare, so get them involved in the kitchen. Initiate the two-bite rule when it comes to food. They don't have to eat everything or like everything, but they have to take at least two bites of each new and unfamiliar food. Remember, their palates are as messed up as yours from years of eating processed foods and it will take time to adjust. Sometimes a new food has to be offered several times and in different ways for it to be enjoyed. If you can't completely clean out your cupboards, at least move their crap out to the garage or to a designated shelf. Ask them if they will please support you in this by eating all junk food and fast food outside the home. Hide fruits and vegetables in their food. Don't let them see you prepare the chocolate spinach smoothie and I guarantee they will love it. And they will never know that the Black Bean Soup has two pounds of greens hidden in it! If you need to eat out occasionally, I will devote a separate section dedicated to that at the end.

Most people do not recognize the cause-effect relationship between diet and health. By the time you are diagnosed with cancer it has been in your body for at least ten years. Just like a smoker does not get lung cancer from smoking cigarettes for a week or a month, the build-up of atherosclerotic plaque in your arteries occurs after years of eating a high fat, high cholesterol diet. My father could never make the connection between his daily angina and daily slice of kosher salami. And when he died after a failed open heart surgery, his death certificate merely stated "coronary artery disease." But as Dr. Esselstyn so eloquently says, "Heart disease need never exist, and if it exists, it need never progress."

If other people don't understand these concepts, you can't let them stop you.

<u>YABBUT # 5 – It's too hard or I have too much stress.</u>

Please reread my life story.

CHAPTER FOUR
Why unprocessed?

Americans consume most of their calories from products made from deceased animals and processed foods and they consume less than ten percent of their calories from the optimal source: fruits and vegetables. The vegetable they do eat most often is a potato, which would be perfectly healthy but for the fact that it is usually a French fried potato or one that has been doused in butter and sour cream or fully loaded with cheese and bacon.

Processed foods and animal products have much in common. Unlike whole plant foods, they are lacking in fiber. Animal products contain no fiber whatsoever and processed food contains little to none. Fiber not only fills you up and slows the rate that sugar is absorbed into the bloodstream, it also acts like little scrubbing brushes cleaning out your colon. Processed food and animal products also contain no water. This makes them both much more calorie dense. Remember that the more calorie rich a food, the more dopamine released and the more you will eat of it. And without the bulk provided by the water and fiber found in whole plant food, you will need to eat many more calories to feel full. We have something in our stomachs called stretch receptors that need to be activated in order for us to feel full. While it is possible to lose weight by portion control, in the long run it won't work because you will eventually give in to hunger. If all you eat is processed foods and animal products, you likely will have to overeat in calories in order to activate those stretch receptors and feel full.

Processed food and animal products also have something else in common. They are both calorie rich and nutrient poor. On the other hand, whole plant foods (with the exception of nuts and seeds) are relatively low in calories and extremely high in nutrients, especially micronutrients. Whole plant foods contain vitamins, minerals, phytochemicals and antioxidants. These are the nutrients you want to consume in quantity if you want to prevent and reverse disease. And you want to consume them in their whole food form, not in the form of supplements. Processed foods and animal products have no phytochemicals or antioxidants and almost no vitamins and minerals.

In addition to having stretch receptors in our stomachs, we also have nutrient receptors in our brains. We can never meet our nutrient needs by eating processed food or animal products because they both are virtually devoid of nutrients. It is possible for someone to be grossly obese and still starving on a cellular level. Until their nutrient needs are met by a diet rich in whole plant food, they will continue to overeat. Unless you are eating a majority of your calories from nuts and seeds, it is virtually impossible to over-consume on a whole food plant-based diet. Simply put, with your nutrient and calorie needs met and your stretch receptors activated, you would be too full.

When your caloric intake is high because of sugar and oil, chances are you will not be meeting your nutrient needs. Let's take a look now at what I dub "The Evil Trinity": sugar, oil, and salt. The more of these three ingredients you eat, especially in concert with each other, the more of them you will want. Let's go over them one at a time.

Sugar: My mother used to say if you don't have something nice to say, say nothing. The American Heart Association—hardly a group of nutritional radicals—says we should consume no more than five percent of our calories from processed sweeteners. For a person consuming two thousand calories a day, that would be a hundred calories or approximately five teaspoons of sugar. With the average can of soda having at least double that amount, how can the average American stay within these guidelines? There is no upside to sugar. It provides nothing but empty calories and is devoid of nutrients. In fact, it is an anti-nutrient, which means it actually ***inhibits*** the absorption of other nutrients.

My students are always trying to convince me that their preferred form of sweetener is healthy. "But what about agave, barley malt, brown rice syrup, brown sugar, cane juice, coconut sugar, evaporated cane juice, fruit juice concentrate, high fructose corn syrup, honey, maple syrup, molasses, palm sugar, yacon syrup and everything else from A-Z?" Unfortunately, just because a sweetener is raw, expensive, organic or blessed by a monk in Tibet does not make it any healthier. Sugar is sugar is sugar is sugar. We could probably make a case that some of these sweeteners are less bad than others, but we can't make the case that any of them are actually healthy. In August of 2010, research at UCLA's Jonsson Cancer Center revealed that it was the fructose in sugar, not the sucrose, that caused cancer cells to proliferate. Some sweeteners like agave are often ninety percent or more fructose, so personally I would avoid those. If you are only using the recommended five teaspoons a day, then I don't think it really matters which one you use, keeping in mind that honey is not vegan and you can't give it to a baby. I love how Jack La Lanne said, "You wouldn't wake up your dog in the morning and give him a cup of coffee, a doughnut and a cigarette, so why do you do that to yourself?" I always figure that if a food is not suitable for a baby or a puppy, maybe we shouldn't be eating it, either.

People often ask about stevia, xylitol, or artificial sweeteners. Stevia is an herb, and unless you are buying it in its whole leaf form, it is processed. So that does not comport with the aim of this book: To help you to avoid, eliminate or at least reduce your consumption of processed food. If you are going to use stevia, I would use the whole leaf instead of the white powder. When you consume things like stevia, xylitol, and any of the sugar alcohols, it just perpetuates your desire for ***more sweet***. Plus, it still stimulates the release of insulin from the pancreas. Avoid artificial sweeteners such as aspartame like the plague. There is a lot of evidence that they are dangerous.

People always want to argue with me that their sweetener is superior, or least not as bad as white sugar. That is like arguing that snorting cocaine is better for you than injecting heroin. It's called rationalization. People aren't seeking the healthiest sweeter so they can sprinkle it on their kale. They are using the sweeteners in conjunction with other unhealthy or low-nutrient foods like flour and oil so they can bake a cake or put some in their liquid drug of choice like coffee or iced tea. They want me to approve of their sweetener so that they can use two cups of it in a recipe and I won't do it. Remember, all sweeteners are highly processed, highly caloric and nutrient poor. We are meant to satisfy our sweet tooth with fruit.

But that doesn't mean you have to desert dessert altogether. You will have several scrumptious, decadent dessert recipes in the recipe section that are sweetened only with dates and other fruits. And I guarantee you these will satisfy your sweet tooth and are as good, or better, as their sugar/oil/salt counterparts. Just try the Raw Orange Chocolate Mousse torte and you'll see what I mean. And if you can't have chocolate, it's just as delicious with carob.

Keep in mind that dates are a high-sugar and low-water fruit. So, while still a better choice, they are quite caloric. A deglet noor date averages about twenty calories and a medjool about forty calories. Still, unlike processed sweeteners, they are a *whole food*, which means they do contain fiber, vitamins, minerals, and antioxidants. The presence of fiber, minerals and other micronutrients in the food slows the spike of glucose in the blood and curtails free radical formation in response to a sugar load. Plus, they taste great. They are like nature's candy. You can also buy date sugar (basically just dehydrated, ground dates, so a whole food), but in my experience it does not dissolve very well, especially in hot liquids. Also, the kind you normally can buy in stores is processed with wheat flour so if you need to avoid wheat or gluten, this wouldn't work. You can buy gluten-free date sugar online. I prefer date paste or date syrup to date sugar.

You will learn how easy and inexpensive it is to make both in the recipe section. If you don't want to make it yourself, you can buy it online at: www.organicsareforeveryone.com.

This product should be available in stores soon. Please keep in mind that even healthier treats made of whole foods are still treats. Eat them mindfully and savor every delicious bite. Think of dates as a transition food in helping you to get off refined sweeteners and do not consume them if you are diabetic.

Oil: Just as all sugar is sugar, all oil is oil. Some oils may, in fact, be worse than others, but no oil is healthy. As with sugar, the only good oil is NONE! Oil is the most fattening food on the planet, weighing in at 4,000 calories a pound. Even nuts and seeds are only 2,800 calories a pound. And chocolate, a mere 2,200 calories a pound☺! Compare this to WHOLE plant food such as fruits and vegetables, which are 100-300 calories a pound. Or compare this to potatoes, beans and grains, which are 400-600 calories per pound. Even avocados are only 750 calories a pound. For the calories in only one mere tablespoon of olive oil, you could consume almost an entire avocado! Which do you think tastes better, would fill up your tummy and satisfy you more? In addition, all oils are almost completely devoid of nutrients!

People always tell me that they read or heard that olive oil is heart healthy and they cite The Mediterranean Heart Study. If you really read the study, you will see that these people on the Island of Crete in the 1950's were healthy ***in spite of*** their consumption of olive oil, not because of it. They were also eating tons of fruits and vegetables and walking many miles a day. It is true that if you switch from using butter to using olive oil, your cholesterol may go down. But take someone like me with a blood cholesterol of 90-110 mg/dl. If I were to start eating oil, my cholesterol would go up! Also, if you read the label on a bottle of oil, you'll see that the recommended serving size is one tablespoon. How many people do you know who eat only one tablespoon per day? The average person will drench his or her otherwise healthy salads or vegetable dishes with at least 400 calories of pure fat. For that many calories, you could eat four pounds of salad, a pound of sweet potatoes or almost two pounds of fruit. Which do you think will fill you up and satisfy you more? And coconut oil, at ninety-two percent saturated fat (the worst kind of fat), is the most dangerous of all and has more saturated fat than even meat!

It is very easy to prepare delicious food without oil. As with salt, in most cases you can simply omit it. Except for frying (and we shouldn't be eating fried foods anyway), any recipe that calls for oil can be made without it and I bet you won't even notice the difference. If you need to sauté, you can use any liquid. Water, fruit juice, vegetable juice, low-sodium vegetable broth, even wine; they all work well. Just make sure you have a good non-stick pan and add the liquid a small amount at a time and be sure not to let the contents in the pan burn. You can even caramelize onions without oil in the oven.

When I adapt dessert recipes, I often use applesauce in place of oil or whole coconut in place of coconut oil. When I roast vegetables in the oven I use a good balsamic vinegar in place of the oil.

Maybe you're still not convinced. After all, I know that popular TV personalities, like Dr. Oz and Rachael Ray, say that olive oil is heart healthy. I know there's a lot of misinformation out there. So let me explain it to you this way. Let's suppose that there is something truly beneficial in say olive oil, coconut oil or flax oil. Would it then not also be there in the WHOLE FOOD FORM, in the olive, the coconut and the flax seed? Are we supposed to believe that something magically happens in the processing of oil that somehow adds these beneficial compounds that were not present in the WHOLE FOOD to begin with? Is this starting to make sense? When you take olives and make olive oil, pretty much everything good about the olive like the fiber, vitamins and minerals is processed out and you're left with the sludge. I want you to eat unprocessed whole food. No oil is a whole food; all oils are highly processed. So eat the olive, not the olive oil. Eat whole coconut (in moderation), never the coconut oil. And eat whole, ground flax seeds, not flax oil. You would be absolutely amazed at how much weight you would lose even if oil were the only thing you took out of your diet.

Keep in mind, in cautioning you about oil, I am *not* telling you not to eat fat. I am telling you that when you do eat fat, eat only whole food fat like nuts, seeds and avocado, and eat them in moderation. Always eat your nuts and seeds raw, not roasted, and unsalted. Kids need fat, but they don't need oil. They can get all the fat their brains need from avocado, nuts, seeds and unsalted nut or seed butter. You can even occasionally eat the richer, higher fat plant foods like tofu and tempeh. Yes, they are minimally processed, so if you want to be a purist just go back to the whole food source and eat the edamame. Edamame in their shell make a delicious and fun snack. Soy and corn are two of the most genetically modified crops so if you are worried about consuming GMO's, make sure you read the label and get a non-GMO brand. I do not recommend the fake meats. They are still very highly processed and isolated soy protein has been shown to be harmful. While it's true that unlike animal products, fake meats have no cholesterol and may be a great transition food, the goal is to be eating whole, unprocessed plant food.

I can't really tell you how much fat you should be eating in your diet as this is a very heated topic, even among the experts. Dr. McDougall, whom I have long admired, generally recommends that we should get no more than ten percent of our calories from fat. He says that nuts, seeds, and avocado and other high fat plant foods are condiments and occasional treats that should only be eaten if we are not overweight. Many of his colleagues agree with him. Dr. Esselstyn, another hero of mine, says if you have heart disease and your LDL is above 80 mg/dl, you should avoid nuts, seeds and avocado. On the other hand, Dr. Fuhrman, from whom I have learned much and whose work steered me in the direction of nutritional excellence, recommends that everyone should have one to two ounces of nuts or seeds per day regardless of their current health or weight. My LDL is 57 mg/dl and I do eat nuts, seeds and avocado. I generally do not eat them by themselves but in recipes. I do not eat them every day but I greatly enjoy them and for me, they make this way of eating even more delicious. When I make guacamole, I generally add one pound of defrosted frozen green peas to the avocados and other ingredients to reduce the amount of fat. I love making salad dressings out of nuts and seeds so I can really enjoy my salads. I have been eating plant-based for thirty-three years and I don't think I could have stayed this way if I completely avoided the richer plant foods.

So, who do you listen to? I get students in my class every single week who are following the programs of one of these nutritional giants. And they constantly ask me, who is right? I don't know. So I always tell them the same thing. Follow the one whose program you can do for the rest of your life. If you look at my diet over several days, it is really a hybrid of all three of these plant diet icons. On some days, you might say I'm more of a McDougaller. On others, I eat more like an Esselstyn (I spent a week with their entire family in Austin, and let me tell you, I have never seen slender people who could eat so much food, especially Ann ☺!). I almost always have a green smoothie for breakfast and a salad for lunch, so if you catch me at those meals you would think that all my meals are Fuhrman-friendly. Our dinners almost always consist of potatoes of one color or another (in honor of McDougall) and a ton of steamed greens a lá Esselstyn.

I almost don't think it matters who is right. I like to look at where they all agree and they all say we should be eating a **whole**

food plant-based diet with no oil and either little or no processed sugar and little or no salt. If everyone did that, disease rates would plummet.

Salt: "But we *need* salt" or "Isn't sea salt *good* for you?" If I had a nickel for every time I heard that, I would be a rich woman. Yes, we require a small amount of sodium, but we can be healthy with as little as 150 mg per day. One teaspoon of salt has 2,400 mg of sodium, so we require merely 1/16 of a teaspoon a day for bodily function. How many people add only 1/16 of a teaspoon of salt a day to their food? The upward recommendation for sodium is 2,300 mg per day. And if you are eating any processed food at all, you are definitely not sodium deficient. How many people do you know who actually are sodium deficient? In addition to raising your blood pressure, high salt consumption is also linked to stroke and stomach cancer.

The more salt you eat, the more salt you want. When you are addicted to salt, you can't really appreciate the amazing flavors of whole foods. Have you ever heard that when someone quits smoking they often gain weight? While there are many reasons that contribute to this, I believe that one of them is that now that they are no longer burning their taste buds with hot tobacco, they can taste and enjoy food again! The same thing happens with salt. Once your palate adjusts, you will be able to taste the inherent saltiness in food. Just as when you give up processed sweeteners, fruit tastes exceedingly sweet, a similar thing occurs with salt. You will notice that even celery tastes salty. My taste buds are so clean now that I can eat a plain baked potato and steamed broccoli with nothing on it and truly enjoy it! Even products labeled "low-sodium" can still be fairly high in sodium. And sometimes they even contain MSG. I used to use low sodium vegetable broth when making soups but I found they were still too high in sodium. Plus, why pay three bucks a carton when water is free? Not flavorful enough for you? You can make your own veggie stock or use fresh vegetable juice, or a combination of juices, as a base. Fresh celery, carrot and tomato juices are my favorites.

If you still crave that salty flavor, there are a few healthier things you can use to simulate a salt flavor. First, I would recommend sea vegetables. There are several varieties like kelp, dulse, nori and kombu that can be purchased in whole sheets. (They say if you cook your beans with a piece of kombu, they won't give you gas.) Smoked dulse is my favorite and I love using chopped pieces of it in salads and oil-free stir-frys. Some of the sea veggies like kelp and dulse also come granulated or powdered so you can sprinkle them on foods as you would salt. Sea vegetables are harvested in the ocean so they are high in minerals and have a naturally salty taste with a fraction of the sodium, roughly 25–35 mg per teaspoon.

You can buy sea vegetables at most heath food stores, but you will get better prices online at www.seaveg.com. You can also find several blends of salt-free seasonings at almost any store. I am not advocating the salt substitutes that contain potassium chloride. I am talking about natural salt-free blends or dried herbs and spices such as *Mrs. Dash*. My favorite, *Benson's Table Tasty*, you can only buy online at: www.bensonsgourmetseasoning.com.

When I worked at the retirement home, the chefs were prohibited from using any salt or salt substitutes. The way they gave their food lots of flavor so that the residents did not miss the salt was by using plenty of other spices (like garlic, cumin and pepper) and lots of fresh herbs (like parsley, basil, thyme, rosemary and cilantro, to name a few). You can always use dried herbs, but in my opinion, fresh tastes best. Adding both the juice and zest from lemons or limes to the finish of your soups and stews and to salad dressings also tricks the palate into thinking there is salt in the dish.

Now it's time for me to bring out the big guns: Sun dried tomatoes. I simply take them and put them in my high-powered blender and make a coarse powder. It is extraordinarily rich and flavorful; you will find it in lots of my recipes. If you don't have a high-powered blender, you can grind them in a small electric coffee grinder, which you can purchase for less than twenty bucks. Just make sure you don't overfill the unit. Use only the oil-free sun dried tomatoes that you usually find in the produce section. They are on the firm or hard side. This technique will not work with the oil-packed kind as you will get a paste and not a powder. Even many regular grocery stores sell bulk sun dried tomatoes in the produce section. If you have a dehydrator, you can easily make your own. You can also buy sun dried tomato powder online and even beet powder made from just beets!

But what about the expensive designer salts like Celtic sea salt or pink Himalayan salt? They have minerals, don't they? While it's true that you may find an almost negligible amount of minerals in sea salt when compared to iodized salt, we aren't supposed to eat salt to get our minerals. That's what green vegetables are for.

If you are used to a high sodium diet, it's true that some of these recipes may taste bland to you for awhile, so here are a few things I do in certain recipes when I am entertaining for "regular people." Instead of salt, I will use either low-sodium miso or low-sodium soy sauce or tamari. Miso, a fermented food used in Japan for centuries to make soup, may have only 110 mg of sodium per teaspoon. (That's what the brand I buy has; some are much, much higher.) Compare 110 mg per teaspoon of miso to 2,400 mg for a teaspoon of salt. You can have almost twenty-four teaspoons of miso for the same amount of sodium, and miso is a rich paste that tastes very salty, so you end up using far less than table salt. When I was in Japan, we had miso soup for breakfast every morning as the Japanese believe that it has many health benefits. Tamari is basically soy sauce that is wheat free—preferable for people who must avoid wheat. The low-sodium tamari has 700 mg of sodium per tablespoon, roughly 233 mg of sodium per teaspoon, which is still way less than the 2,400 mg in a teaspoon of salt. Trader Joe's low-sodium soy sauce (which is not wheat-free) contains only 460 mg of sodium per tablespoon, roughly 153 mg of sodium per teaspoon, still a far cry from the 2,400 mg in a teaspoon of salt. So remember, if you still insist on using salt, at least don't cook with it. Add it judiciously to the surface of your food where the taste buds on the tip of your tongue can really taste it. But first see if you can skip the salt altogether, especially if you already have high blood pressure.

CHAPTER FIVE

Yes, I want to do this but I don't know how to start.

My first recommendation is that you experiment with an unprocessed diet for just thirty days to assess how you feel, knowing that at the end of the thirty days you can go back to eating whatever you want. Compare how you feel while eating unprocessed whole food to how you felt eating a processed food diet. I have never had one person come back and tell me that after the initial period of detox and withdrawal, he or she actually felt better eating processed food.

I recommend the thirty day trial period because I think something happens in our brains when we think something is forever. I know that's what happened to me when I tried to give up my former addiction, chocolate. It was the worst month of my husband's life! So don't even think about doing this for thirty days if that causes you too much anxiety. Think of doing it for a week or a day or even a meal at a time. Instead of thinking about what you are giving up, think about what you are going towards.

People often make fun of me for eating this way, with little jabs like, "You're really not going to live any longer, it will just *seem* longer." But the truth is that I actually prefer eating this way. I love rarely having to go to the doctor. I love almost never getting sick. I love not having to take dangerous, expensive, ineffective medications to lower my blood pressure, cholesterol, or blood sugar—drugs that often, in the end, only make people sicker. Think about what your quality of life can be if you improve your health. Think about being around to walk your son or daughter down the aisle, or for the birth of your first grandchild.

So, are you starting to see the possibility here of a new you? Are you starting to get excited? Then let's talk about how to start. The first thing I recommend is to clean out all the crap from your cabinets and refrigerator. I've sometimes helped people do this as they cry and scream. Usually, once I clean out someone's kitchen, there is nothing left that I would consider food, so I take them shopping. You need to get rid of all processed food. I define processed food as pretty much anything that comes in a can, a box, a bottle or a bag. If it's not a whole food, then it's a processed food. All oils, all sugars, and all alcohol is processed. Generally, if it's got more than a few ingredients, it's processed. I do make an exception for sugar-free low sodium condiments like ketchup and mustard, salt-free canned beans, and unsweetened non-dairy milks without added sugar or oil. You can actually easily make these milks yourself, but keeping some packaged ones on hand is fine.

Once you truly understand that processed food is not food, this will be so much easier. You may love it, you may be addicted to it, and you may choose to eat it (only occasionally I hope), but it is not food. Most of what is sold in a grocery store is neither whole nor food.

There is a popular vegan restaurant in Los Angeles called Real Food Daily. I love that name because people need to learn that they must eat real food and eat it daily. You must eat food, whole food, and nothing but the whole food. A whole food is something that is grown in nature, not manufactured in a laboratory. Since most of us don't grow our own food, think of a whole food as pretty much anything you can find in the produce section. **If it's not a fruit, vegetable, seed, nut, bean, whole grain, starchy vegetable or legume, then it's not a whole food, it's a processed food**.

Trust me, you don't want processed crap around you, tempting you and contaminating the good food you are about to bring into your home. Think of it like bringing a new baby home; you'd make sure everything was spotless first, wouldn't you? If you are going to "cheat," do so only outside of your home. Never have these foods in your home. The temptation is too great. If it's there, it will sing to you and you will eat it! Please do not think you can rely on willpower alone. Don't sabotage yourself. If you were a recovering alcoholic, would you get a job at a bar? All non-food items must be consumed outside of your home. If you have to leave your home to eat them, you will become infinitely more aware of your addictive patterns and mindless eating. Eat ***mindfully.*** And if you do fall off the horse, get right back on with the very next bite of food you put into your mouth.

So now that you know the rules, it's time to play the game. Let's go shopping. Let's start in the produce section where the sky is the limit. Buy whatever looks good to you. I often buy what appeals to me visually, like rainbow chard or purple kale. But I also use my nose, especially with fruit, and buy whatever smells good. You can also ask the produce person for help in selecting the ripest fruits. You can even buy fruit already cut up, but it will be more expensive. Make sure you buy plenty of ripe bananas. They freeze great and you can use them in smoothies and make ice cream out of them.

Since there will be no limit placed on the amount of fruits and vegetables you can eat, buy as much as you think you will be able to eat until the next time you can go shopping. Make sure you buy some citrus fruits like lemons, limes, and oranges. They are great for squeezing over a salad, making oil-free dressings, and for use in lots of the recipes. Eat from the rainbow and buy vegetables of every color, such as red bell pepper, yellow squash and purple cabbage. My favorite things to put in a salad are raw, shredded beets. You will also want to buy some sun dried tomatoes which are usually located in this section. Make sure you buy the kind that are oil and salt-free and have no sulfites added. Sulfites are a preservative that many people (like myself) are allergic to and can even trigger migraines and asthma attacks. Make sure you buy some starchy vegetables too, like peas or corn and some potatoes of any color. Most of what you will eat and buy will be from the produce section, so be very careful when venturing out to the rest of the store unattended.

Next, go to the frozen food section and buy frozen fruit for your smoothies. My favorite is cherries. Make sure they do not have sugar added. Also stock up on your favorite frozen vegetables. If you don't think you will make your own non-dairy milk, or to have some on hand in case of emergency, buy a few boxes. Almond milk is my favorite, but if you are allergic to nuts you can buy hemp milk, rice milk, soy milk, or oat milk. I have never seen a brand yet that doesn't have added sodium, so if you want to be a purist you can make your own with the recipe in this book. I like the vanilla flavored milks and *Blue Diamond* even makes a chocolate one with no added sugar.

If you like, check out the salad dressing section. Personally, I have never found a bottled oil-free salad dressing that I really loved, but if you can find one that you love, go ahead and buy it. It will probably have added sugar and way too much sodium, but have a bottle on hand for emergencies. Our "emergency" salad dressing for when we travel and can't make our own is *Newman's Own Low Fat Sesame Ginger*. It is by no means perfect but it works in a pinch and we use only a little. We want you to love your salad so it's really important that your dressing be delicious. Other things that make great dressings are oil-free hummus, guacamole and Pico de Gallo salsa.

Finally, end your healthy shopping trip with a visit to the bulk section and buy your favorite beans and grains. Quinoa (technically a seed, not a grain) is my favorite but you can also buy oats, rice, barley, and a plethora of other grains. Most grains are also available in boxes. They are more expensive that way but if you've never cooked them before it's a great way to start out because the directions will be on the package. And if you don't want to cook your beans, you can always buy salt-free beans in a can. Even if you do cook your own beans, these are good to have on hand.

Feel free to browse the spice aisle and buy any spices or extracts that tickle your fancy. You can also buy fresh herbs in the produce section. The only other thing I buy ready-made is something called a *Lara Bar*. It is made of dried fruit and nuts only. While higher in calories than the other foods you'll be eating with abandon, they are great for traveling as they do not need to be refrigerated. Read labels because some flavors of *Lara Bars* now have coconut oil or sugar, so choose the flavors that are comprised of just fruits and nuts. And if you are one of those people who just can't eat nuts and dried fruit in moderation, don't buy them. Feel free to buy flax seeds, though, and put a tablespoon in your smoothies or on your salads to get all your essential fatty acids. Flax seeds have to be ground first to be assimilated so if you don't have a coffee grinder or blender you can always buy them already ground. Just be sure to keep them in the refrigerator as they can easily turn rancid.

What about alcohol, you ask? Well, from a nutrient standpoint, like oil and sugar, alcohol has no nutrients, just calories. And it is almost twice as fattening as sugar and almost as fattening as oil. Sugar has four calories per gram, alcohol seven calories per gram and oil nine calories per gram. In addition, most people eat more when they consume alcohol, and usually it is more of the already unhealthy foods. Yes, you hear of the occasional study that attributes some health benefit to alcohol, taken in moderation. But as with the oil, if there truly is something beneficial in the wine, it was also in the grapes that it was made from. So again, **eat the whole food!** The answer is always in the whole food.

If you still drink coffee, I know how hard that can be to give up, so I might not even think about doing that until you have superior nutrition under your belt for several months. Many people enroll in my Challenge (thirty days on an unprocessed diet—which I now offer remotely) just to give up caffeine and they have all been successful. Remember, coffee is a drug, so you may need some help to come off it. Try drinking your regular coffee with half decaf for a while until you can titrate down to the lowest dose. If you still need the caffeine, switch to green tea. Green smoothies give me all the energy I need to start the day off right.

The only beverage I recommend is water. Just as human beings are the only species to drink milk after maturity and are the only species to drink the lactation fluids of another mammal, we are also the only species to drink, after maturity, any beverage other than water. You often hear that the amount of water you should drink is half of your weight in ounces. If you are eating water-rich foods like fruits and vegetables, you may not need that much. Caffeine is dehydrating so if you are still using it, you will need to drink even more water. They say that once you are thirsty you are already dehydrated, so make sure you never reach that point. And always adjust your fluid intake according to the weather and the amount of exercise you do. I really don't recommend juices unless they are freshly squeezed vegetable juices. And never, ever, drink liquid meat (dairy). Cow's milk was made for a baby calf to grow 800 pounds in a year. It is not fit for human consumption. Milk does a body no good.

Eating out

It is hard enough eating out on a plant-based diet, let alone a whole food plant-based diet free of sugar, salt and oil. But it can be done. First, let's talk a little bit about restaurants. Please keep in mind that like the processed food industry, restaurants are in business to make a profit. Remember, the more salt in food, the more of it you will eat. So restaurants use more salt than you could imagine. Way more salt than you would ever cook with at home. So unless you are ordering a plain salad, a plain baked potato, steamed vegetables or fruit, the likelihood of getting a salt-free or even reduced sodium meal at a restaurant is slim to none. When you ask chefs to prepare food without salt, they look at you as if you are about to cut off their arms. And it is not their fault. Culinary schools do not teach their students how to prepare food salt-free. Even if they did, the vast majority of people who frequent restaurants either do not eat this way or do not expect to when they dine out. So know that when you eat out you are probably going to ingest way more sodium than you would like. Just like the processed food industry, restaurants also use the perfect combination of sugar, fat, and salt that will keep you coming back for more. And the portion size at many restaurants (like *Cheesecake Factory* and *Chili's*) is enough to feed a family of four.

The same goes for oil. Since the majority of the public still believes all the hype about olive oil being "good for your heart" and since chefs do not learn to cook without it in culinary school, pretty much everything in a restaurant is cooked in oil or with oil. Most food in a restaurant is prepped ahead of time and is not cooked to order. Again, if you order nothing but the four items I suggested above, you won't even have to worry about oil. But if you want something a bit more exciting, my advice is to call the restaurant ahead of time and ask them if the chef can accommodate your special dietary needs. Almost all restaurants have their menus online now, so you can look them up and see what dishes look good to you. Then call the restaurant during non-peak hours and ask if they can be of service. Please don't wait until you arrive and the restaurant is already busy and crowded. Most chefs are happy to accommodate you with a bit of advance notice.

The first homework assignment in our "Unprocessed 30 Day Challenge" is to go online and look up the nutritional information for one of the restaurants you frequent and highlight what you usually order. When people actually see the amount of saturated fat, calories and sodium in their food choices, they often make better choices. All chain restaurants are required to have this information available. *Chipotle*, the fast food Mexican chain, is a great one to work with for this example because you can customize your burrito, taco or bowl on-line as you would at the restaurant. Even small changes like omitting the sour cream and cheese lead to huge decreases in the amount of fat and calories. And having everything in a bowl over lettuce and rice instead of on a white flour tortilla or a fried taco shell can reduce the fat and calories even further.

You will generally have better luck at restaurants that allow you to customize your meal. At sandwich shops like *Subway*, *Togo's* and *Quizno's,* you can get everything as a salad or wrap. If you want the bread, make sure they load it with double veggies and no cheese or mayo. Ask for mustard or low-fat dressing and avocado if you want to live dangerously like me. At Chinese restaurants you can always get steamed rice and steamed veggies. You can request that no oil be used, but there's no guarantee. Many restaurants are really trying to have healthier options available. At *Sharky's*, a Mexican fast food restaurant on the West Coast, they offer organic low-fat whole wheat tortillas, organic brown rice and organic pinto beans. You can even get my favorite, steamed broccoli, on your burrito! And they have an exquisite fire-roasted salsa! *Hugo's* restaurant, with several locations in Southern California, has several healthier options now. Dale Jaffe, a consultant for the restaurant, has taken my classes and has implemented some amazing oil-free vegan options on the menu that Chef Nabor executes perfectly. So change is happening, albeit slowly.

Virtually everyone who has taken my 30 Day Challenge or adopted an unprocessed diet as a lifestyle has reported extraordinary results. Mark lost twenty pounds and lowered his cholesterol by 70 points, completely reversed his Type 2 diabetes, and went off his medication. Wolfie lost forty pounds and started wearing pants without an elastic waist. Pamela had been told by her doctor that she would have to go on statins, but instead went on the Challenge, lost twenty pounds and got her cholesterol under 150 mg/dl. Stacie got off sugar, caffeine, and alcohol. My sister, Barbara, went from a size 14 to a size 4 in seven months and got her cholesterol and triglycerides to within normal limits. The list goes on and on. I don't know anyone who has regretted trying an unprocessed diet.

Keep in mind, many of these common diseases caused by our poor food choices are far easier to prevent than they are to treat. But many of them still can be reversed and it's too late only if you don't start now. The world is not set up optimally to support people who want to eat healthfully, but there are more and more of us willing to lend a hand. Still, this is something you must do largely for yourself, by yourself. Try eating unprocessed for just thirty days and see how you feel. What you will experience in terms of increased energy, vitality and improved health will far outweigh any inconvenience. As they often say at OHI, "Just do your best and bless the rest."

I hope reading my story has inspired you to make some changes in the direction of optimum health. If I can do anything to support you in your journey, please write to me at chefaj@att.net.

William Jennings Bryan once said, "Never be afraid to stand with the minority when the minority is right, for the minority which is right will one day be the majority."

Welcome to the minority.

Love & Kale, Chef AJ

Over 100 Whole Food

Plant Indulgent

RECIPES

Without sugar, oil or salt.

One of the best things about eating an unprocessed, oil-free, nutrient-rich, whole food, plant-based diet is that unless you are overdoing the whole food fats like avocado, coconut, nuts and seeds, you can pretty much eat all the food you desire. That is why we elected not to include the serving sizes and nutritional information in the recipe section. When you are eating exclusively fruits, vegetables, beans, legumes, whole grains and starchy vegetables (and no more than one to two ounces of nuts or seeds) every day, there is no need for counting calories or weighing or measuring your food. If you eat when hungry, stop when full, and don't eat animal products or refined and processed food (or if you must, keeping their intake to less than 10% of your total calories), you will no longer be obsessed with counting anything. And although we didn't mention it, we think exercise is important too. But as Dr. Caldwell B. Esselstyn, Jr. says, "Diet trumps everything." With these recipes we know that you will be able to enjoy food that comes from plants, instead of a manufacturing plant.

DECADENT DESSERTS

Life is uncertain.
Eat DESSERT first.

BANANA STRAWBERRY MOUSSE TART

(Raw)

This is equally delicious when made with raw carob powder.

INGREDIENTS: (Crust)
1 cup raw cashews or macadamia nuts
1 cup unsweetened dried coconut
2 cups pitted dates
1 Tablespoon alcohol-free vanilla

METHOD: (Crust)
In a food processor fitted with the "S" blade, process the nuts into a powder. Add coconut and process again. Add enough dates until mixture holds together when formed into a ball. Add vanilla and process again. Press mixture evenly onto the bottom of a fluted tart pan.

INGREDIENTS: (Filling)
2 large ripe avocados
1/3 cup raw cacao powder or carob powder
1 cup date paste or more or less, to taste
1 Tablespoon alcohol-free vanilla
Sliced ripe bananas and strawberries

METHOD: (Filling) In a food processor fitted with the "S" blade, process first 4 ingredients until smooth. Spread half the filling on the crust and place sliced bananas on top. Layer the other half of the filling on the bananas and place the sliced strawberries on top. Chill and serve with Raspberry Coulis (page 73).

BASIC HEALTHY PIE CRUST

(Raw)

Super easy to make and the varieties are endless.

INGREDIENTS:
2 cups raw nuts
2 cups pitted dates

METHOD:
In a food processor fitted with the "S" blade, process the nuts until they are a flour-like consistency. Do not over-process or you will have a nut butter. Add dates, a few at a time, until the mixture clumps together. Stop the machine and if you can easily roll a ball from the mixture and it sticks together, you don't need to add any more dates. Press the crust into a pie plate, tarte pan or springform pan. It's great just topped with cut up fresh fruits of any kind. You can even roll the mixture into balls and you have healthy cookies. Play around with adding different spices (like cinnamon or nutmeg), different extracts (like vanilla or almond), or the zest and juice of lemons, limes or oranges.

Chef's Note: Substitute raw seeds (such as hemp, sesame, pumpkin or sunflower) for all or some of the nuts. Substitute dried fruit (such as apricots, cherries, cranberries, currants, figs, prunes, raisins) for all or some of the dates.

BERRIED TREASURES

(Raw)

My friend, Tim Ray, loves these even more than chocolate!

INGREDIENTS: (Crust)
2 cups raw walnuts
2 cups pitted dates

METHOD: (Crust)
In a food processor fitted with the "S" blade, process nuts into a powder. Do not over-process them into a nut butter. Add dates a few at a time until mixture sticks together so you can easily roll it into a ball.

INGREDIENTS: (Filling)
2 pounds frozen blueberries, defrosted
1 pound dates, soaked in 16 ounces of orange juice
Juice and zest of one lemon (about 1/4 cup of juice)
2 Tablespoons psyllium husks

METHOD: (Filling)
In a food processor fitted with the "S" blade, puree blueberries and dates until smooth. Add lemon and psyllium husks and process again briefly.

INGREDIENTS: (Streusel Topping)
1 cup raw pecans
1 cup unsweetened coconut
2 cups dates
2 teaspoons cinnamon
1/2 teaspoon nutmeg

METHOD: (Streusel Topping)

In a food processor fitted with the "S" blade, process nuts into a flour, being careful not to over-process and turn them into a nut butter. Add the coconut, cinnamon, and nutmeg and process again. Add dates, a few at a time, until a streusel-like texture is achieved.

ASSEMBLY:

Press crust into the bottom of an 8 inch square springform pan. Pour filling over crust. Sprinkle topping over blueberry filling. There may be extra topping left. Reserve for another use such as sprinkling on fresh fruit. Chill until firm, cut into squares.

Chef Notes: Substitute blackberries and/or raspberries for all or some of the blueberries. These freeze well and are also delicious warmed. For an extra-decadent treat, serve with Macadamia Nut Crème (page 68) or Pear Crème Anglais (page 72).

CARAMEL APPLES

(Raw)

When I gave up processed and refined sweeteners, I never thought I would be able to enjoy a caramel apple again. Then I created this. Why wait for the fall or Halloween when you can enjoy this healthy treat any time of year? They look just like the real thing and kids of all ages love them!

INGREDIENTS:

Date paste (page 65)
Apples
Sticks

I loved + Marc def. liked even w/ coconut. Got caramel extract from Walmart. I rolled in nibs, coconut + crushed mixed nuts. Very tasty treat!

METHOD:
Make date paste according to the recipe (page 65) but add 1 teaspoon of caramel extract.
Place apple upside down on a flat surface and push stick into the center. Roll the apple in date paste using your hands, if necessary, to get it to stick over the entire surface of the apple. Roll in your favorite topping such as nuts, cacao nibs, unsweetened coconut, Goji berries, or a combination. Chill well before serving.

Chef's Note: Sticks for caramel apples can be found at craft stores or cake decorating stores. If you have trouble finding them, slice apple into wedges and make individual dipped apple slices. Also great dipped into the streusel topping (page 74).

CHERRIED TREASURES

(Raw)

Frozen cherries aren't always available so when you see them, be sure to stock up.

INGREDIENTS: (Crust)
2 cups raw walnuts
1 cup pitted dates
1 cup dried unsweetened cherries

METHOD: (Crust)
In a food processor fitted with the "S" blade, process nuts into a powder. Do not over-process them into a nut butter. Add dates and dried cherries a few at a time until mixture sticks together so you can easily roll it into a ball.

INGREDIENTS: (Filling)
2 pounds frozen cherries, defrosted
1 pound dates, soaked in 16 ounces of orange juice
Juice and zest of two limes (approximately 1/4 cup of juice)
2 Tablespoons psyllium husks

METHOD: (Filling)
In a food processor fitted with the "S" blade, puree cherries and dates until smooth. Add lemon and psyllium and process again briefly.

INGREDIENTS: (Streusel Topping)
1 cup raw pecans
1 cup unsweetened coconut
2 cups dates
2 teaspoons cinnamon
1/2 teaspoon nutmeg

METHOD: (Topping)
In a food processor fitted with the "S" blade, process nuts into a flour being careful not to over process and turn them into a nut butter. Add the coconut, cinnamon, and nutmeg and process again. Add dates, a few at a time, until a streusel-like texture is achieved.

ASSEMBLY:
Press crust into the bottom of an 8 inch square springform pan. Pour filling over crust. Sprinkle over cherry filling. There may be extra topping left, reserve for another use such as sprinkling on fresh fruit. Chill until firm, cut into squares.

Chef's Note: When you buy dried fruit, always buy a brand that's not only free of added sugar and oil, but also sulfite-free. Many people are sensitive to sulfites, which are often used as a preservative. In sensitive people, it can trigger asthma or migraines. It's also fun to make this a layered dessert by doing one layer of blueberry with one layer of cherry on top! You can also soak the dates in pomegranate juice instead of orange juice.

CHERRY COBBLER

(Raw)

This tastes as good as it looks and is also delicious warmed in the dehydrator.

INGREDIENTS: (Filling)
3 x 16 ounce bags frozen cherries, thawed and drained
1 cup pitted dates, soaked in the cherry juice from draining
juice and rind of 1 lemon
1 Tablespoon alcohol-free vanilla extract

METHOD: (Filling)
In a food processor fitted with the "S" blade, process about 1/4 of the thawed cherries with the rest of the ingredients. Stir this mixture into the remaining cherries by hand. Chill 1 hour or until firm.

INGREDIENTS: (Streusel Topping)
1 cup raw pecans
1 cup unsweetened coconut
2 cups dates
2 teaspoons cinnamon
1/2 teaspoon nutmeg

METHOD: (Streusel Topping)
In a food processor fitted with the "S" blade, process nuts into a flour, being careful not to over-process and turn them into a nut butter. Add the coconut, cinnamon, and nutmeg and process again. Add dates, a few at a time, until a streusel-like texture is achieved.

ASSEMBLY:
In a parfait glass, alternate layering the cherry filling with the streusel topping. Top with Macadamia Nut Crème (page 68).

Chef's Note: Substitute fresh or frozen peaches for all or some of the cherries.

CHOCOLATE GLAZED BALSAMIC STRAWBERRIES

A simple, yet elegant, easy to prepare dessert.

INGREDIENTS:
1 pound strawberries, stems removed and sliced in quarters
2 Tablespoons chocolate-infused balsamic vinegar
(or 1 Tablespoon vinegar plus 1 Tablespoon date syrup)
1/4 cup finely chopped fresh mint and raw cacao nibs

METHOD:
Mix vinegar and date syrup, if using. Add mint. Pour over sliced strawberries and let marinate several hours in the refrigerator, stirring occasionally. Place in parfait glasses and sprinkle with cacao nibs before serving.

Chef's Note: You can also use regular balsamic vinegar.

CHOCOLATE FUNDUE

I created this dip as a way to get my friend's 4 year old to eat fruit.

INGREDIENTS:
1 cup peanut butter (no salt or sugar)
1 cup date paste
1/2 cup raw cacao powder (or carob powder)
3/4-1 cup unsweetened non-dairy milk (until desired thickness is reached)
1 Tablespoon alcohol-free vanilla extract
1/2 teaspoon caramel extract (optional)

METHOD:
Place all ingredients except the milk in a food processor fitted with the "S" blade and process until ingredients are incorporated, scraping down sides if necessary. Slowly add non-dairy milk, a little at a time until desired consistency is reached. You can eat this immediately or chill for a firmer texture.

Chef's Note: Serve this as a dip with your favorite fruit such as cut apples or strawberries. Or buy wooden skewers and place several different fruits on it shish kabob style. If you have leftover FUNdue, make Nutty Buddies (page 71) or Peanut Butter Fudge Truffles (page 170). You can make a raw version of this by using raw almond butter or tahini. To drastically reduce the fat, my friend Robin replaces half the nut butter with drained and rinsed cannellini beans. You could probably even add more beans and less nut butter and still keep the flavor. If you don't do chocolate or carob, you can make a Creamy Peanut Butter dip.

DATE PASTE

(Raw)

Make sure you always have some on hand to create a healthy dessert in no time.

INGREDIENTS:
1 pound pitted dates
1 cup liquid (water, unsweetened non-dairy milk, or unsweetened juice)

METHOD:
Soak dates in liquid overnight or for several hours until much of the liquid is absorbed. In food processor fitted with the "S" blade, process dates and liquid until completely smooth. Store date paste in the refrigerator.

DATE SYRUP

Great to use in place of maple syrup.

INGREDIENTS:
Pitted dates
Water

METHOD:
Place dates in a saucepan and cover with water. Softer dates will break down more easily. Bring the water to a boil. Let it boil for 5 minutes, and then put it on a the lowest heat and simmer for 30-60 minutes, depending on if your dates are very soft or hard. Let the mixture cool. Once cooled, add the mixture to a blender and blend until very smooth.

Chef's Note: You can also purchase date syrup at: www.organicsareforeveryone.com

D.B.'s SPECIAL

(Raw)

Whoever thought a salad could be a dessert? Well now it can! This salad was created by "accident" by my friend Michelle Wolf's niece D.B. who put the streusel topping from the Berried Treasures on a salad.

INGREDIENTS: (Salad)
Fresh beets
Carrots
Apples

METHOD:
In a food processor fitted with the shredding blade, shred equal amounts of all three ingredients and place in a large bowl.

INGREDIENTS: (Mango Orange Sauce)
8 ounces frozen mango, defrosted (or equivalent amount of fresh, ripe mango)
1/2 cup orange juice
1/8 cup fresh lime juice
1/2 teaspoon cinnamon

METHOD:
Place all dressing ingredients in a high-powered blender and blend until smooth. Pour over salad and mix well. Top with Streusel Topping (page 74).

Chef's Note: If you don't have a food processor, you could shred all of the ingredients by hand. It will just take much longer.

HOCKEY PUCKS

I remember reading in Dr. Caldwell B. Esselstyn, Jr.'s book "Prevent and Reverse Heart Disease" that he eats 8 peanut butter cups every New Year's Eve. When I had the honor of having him at my home for dinner, I created this recipe so he could enjoy them more than once a year. I originally called them "Essies" in his honor but Ann Wheat, owner of the amazing Millennium Restaurant in San Francisco, renamed them Hockey Pucks because of their shape.

INGREDIENTS: (Filling)
1 cup date paste
1 cup peanut butter, unsweetened and unsalted
1 Tablespoon alcohol-free vanilla

METHOD:
In a food processor fitted with the "S" blade, process date paste, peanut butter and vanilla until smooth and creamy. Add a little unsweetened almond milk if mixture does not process easily. Place filling in a 24-piece silicone brownie pan (available at www.wilton.com) and freeze until firm. Once hard, place coating around filling and freeze.

INGREDIENTS: (Coating)
2 cups unsalted peanuts
1/2 cup raw cacao powder
2 cups pitted dates
1 Tablespoon alcohol-free vanilla

METHOD:
In a food processor fitted with the "S" blade, grind peanuts into a powder. Add cacao powder and process again briefly. Add enough dates until mixture sticks together so you can form a ball. Add vanilla and process again. Place coating around each frozen peanut butter square and form into a "hockey puck" with your hands.

Chef's Note: For an all-raw version of these treats, substitute raw almond butter for the peanut butter and raw almonds for the peanuts.

MACADAMIA NUT CRÈME

(Raw)

INGREDIENTS:
2 cups macadamia nuts, soaked in water for at least an hour
Date Paste (page 65), to taste
1 Tablespoon alcohol-free vanilla extract
1/2 teaspoon almond extract

METHOD:
In a high-powered blender, blend the soaked cashews with as little water as possible. Add the dates and extract, adding more water if necessary to get a thick, but smooth, creamy topping which is delicious on everything, especially fruit desserts.

Chef's Note: Substitute raw cashews for the macadamia nuts and orange juice for the water.

MINT CHOCOLATE MOUSSE TORTE

A healthier version of the Frango Mint Pie I ate at as a child at Marshall Field's in Chicago.

INGREDIENTS: (Filling)
16 ounces pitted dates, soaked in 16 ounces unsweetened chocolate almond milk
12 ounces walnuts
1/2 cup raw cacao powder
1/2 cup unsweetened coconut
1 Tablespoon alcohol-free vanilla extract
1-2 teaspoons peppermint extract (depending on how minty you like it)
1/2 cup raw cacao nibs

METHOD: (Filling)
In a food processor fitted with the "S" blade, process soaked dates and extracts until very smooth. Add cacao powder and process again until smooth. Place this in a bowl. Then process the nuts into a nut butter-like consistency. Add coconut and process again. Add this to the date mixture and stir well by hand until all of the ingredients are completely incorporated. Pour over crust and freeze until firm. Garnish with raw cacao nibs.

INGREDIENTS: (Crust)
2 cups raw walnuts
2 cups pitted dates
1/4 cup raw cacao powder
1 Tablespoon alcohol-free vanilla
1 teaspoon peppermint extract

METHOD: (Crust)
In a food processor fitted with the "S" blade, process the nuts into a powder. Do not over process or you will have a nut butter. Add dates, a few at a time, until the mixture clumps together. Stop the machine and if you can easily roll a ball from the mixture and it sticks together you don't need to add anymore dates. Add extracts and process again briefly. Press the crust into a springform pan. Spread filling over the top and freeze until solid.

MANGO ORANGE SAUCE

A simple dressing for fruit or salad.

INGREDIENTS:
8 ounces frozen mango, defrosted (or equivalent amount of fresh, ripe mango)
1/2 cup orange juice
1/8 cup fresh lime juice
1/2 teaspoon cinnamon

METHOD:
Place all dressing ingredients in a high powered blender and blend until smooth.

Chef's Note: Frozen fruits can be as nutritious as fresh because they are picked at their peak and flash frozen. It's a good idea to have your freezer filled with a variety of frozen fruit.

NUTTY BUDDIES

Tastes just like the frozen bananas from Disneyland, but you won't have to Mickey Mouse around with your health.

INGREDIENTS: One batch of Chocolate FUNdue (page 64)

METHOD:
Place a stick in a peeled, ripe banana and coat it with the mixture, using your hands, if necessary, to coat evenly. Roll the banana in chopped nuts or unsweetened coconut. Freeze on wax paper.

Chef's Note: If you don't have sticks, slice the banana and make individual pieces.

ORANGE CHOCOLATE MOUSSE TORTE

(Raw)

This is the first recipe I created after culinary school and it's sold at the restaurant where I work today.

One recipe of Basic Healthy Pie Crust (page 57) to which 1/4 cup raw cacao powder has been added.

INGREDIENTS: (Filling)
16 ounces pitted dates soaked in 16 ounces orange juice
12 ounces walnuts
1/2 cup raw cacao powder (or carob powder)
1/2 cup unsweetened coconut
1 Tablespoon alcohol-free vanilla extract
1 teaspoon orange extract (optional)

METHOD:
In a food processor fitted with the "S" blade, process soaked dates and extracts until very smooth. Add cacao powder and process again until smooth. Place this in another bowl. Then process the nuts into a nut butter like consistency. Add coconut and process again. Add this to the date mixture and stir well by hand until all of the ingredients are completely incorporated. Pour over crust and freeze until firm. Garnish with raw cacao nibs and flaked coconut.

Chef's Note: I prefer to make this in a springform pan and serve it with Raspberry Coulis (page 73).

PEAR CRÈME ANGLAIS

Xanthan gum is a polysaccharide which is used as a thickener. Leave it out if you wish.

INGREDIENTS:
1 – 28 ounce jar of pears in their own juice
1/3 cup raw cashews or macadamia nuts
1 Tablespoon alcohol-free vanilla extract
1 teaspoon xanthan gum

METHOD:
Drain pears, reserve juice for another use. In a blender, blend pears until smooth. Add remaining ingredients and blend until incorporated. Chill. Serve over fruit desserts.

Chef's Note: Substitute unsweetened jarred peaches in their own juice for the pears.

RASPBERRY COULIS

(Raw)

This sauce is boss!

INGREDIENTS:
1 bag frozen raspberries, defrosted
Date paste, to taste

METHOD:
Puree defrosted fruit and date paste blender until smooth. Add more date paste until desired sweetness is reached. You can also add a teaspoon of alcohol-free vanilla extract, a dash of almond extract, and a little lemon juice, if desired. Pour into a squeeze bottle and serve over any dessert or use in smoothies.

Chef's Note: Other frozen fruits like cherries or strawberries are equally delicious. You can also use fresh fruit.

STREUSEL TOPPING

(Raw)

I always like to keep some on hand to sprinkle over fresh fruit. This can even turn a sliced banana into a special treat.

INGREDIENTS:
1 cup raw pecans
1 cup unsweetened coconut
2 cups pitted dates
2 teaspoons cinnamon
1/2 teaspoon nutmeg

METHOD:
In a food processor fitted with the "S" blade, process nuts into a flour being careful not to over process and turn them into a nut butter. Add the coconut, cinnamon, and nutmeg and process again. Add dates, a few at a time, until a streusel-like texture is achieved. Store in a sealed container in the refrigerator.

Chef's Note: While the ingredients in the streusel topping are basically the same as those in the Basic Healthy Pie Crust, we are looking for an entirely different texture. (That's why I love doing classes and DVDs so you can see what I am talking about). When making a crust, you want everything to stick together and form a ball so that you can press it into a pie pan. When making the streusel topping, you want it more crumbly, so that you can sprinkle it over things like a topping. Some varieties of dates are moister and stickier than others, so be careful not to add so many so that a ball forms. When making a pie crust, however, you do want a ball to form in the food processor.

WICKED FUDGE SAUCE

This is delicious over fresh banana ice cream made with a Champion juicer.

INGREDIENTS:
1 cup raw almond butter
1/2 cup date syrup, or more to taste
1/2 cup raw cacao powder or carob powder
1/2 cup unsweetened non-dairy milk

METHOD:
In a food processor using the "S" blade, process all ingredients until smooth. If you want a thinner sauce, use more non-dairy milk. If you have a high-powered blender, this will become heated and taste like hot fudge.

Chef's Note: If you have a dehydrator, try dehydrating the leftover sauce. You can spread it thin on the Teflex sheets and it will taste like chocolate fruit leather.

AppeTEASERS

A BETTER BRUSCHETTA

This is such a yummy salsa you could even eat it over pasta.

INGREDIENTS:
1 and 1/2 pounds Roma tomatoes, chopped (approximately 5-6)
1 red bell pepper, chopped (approximately 8 ounces)
1 -14 ounce can artichoke hearts in water, rinsed, drained and chopped
3 cloves garlic, peeled and pressed
1/2 cup chopped red onion
1 cup fresh basil, chopped
1/2 cup fresh Italian parsley, chopped
2 Tablespoons balsamic vinegar
2 Tablespoons sun dried tomato powder*

METHOD:
Place all ingredients together in a large bowl and mix well. Serve with baked whole wheat pita chips. (Whole wheat pita is not gluten-free.)

Chef's Note: You can certainly chop all of the ingredients by hand, or you can place ALL of the ingredients in a large bowl and use a chopping tool like an ulu or mezzaluna and chop them all together at once. A food processor is not recommended. It will make everything too watery.

*You can buy sun dried tomato powder online or make your own. Simply buy the sun dried tomatoes that are free of oil, salt and sulfites and grind them in a coffee grinder or high-powered blender.

BAKED TORTILLA CHIPS

Make sure you get tortillas that are made only of corn or just corn and lime.

INGREDIENTS:
Corn tortillas (I like the blue corn ones from Trader Joe's)

METHOD:
Preheat oven to 400 degrees F. Cut each tortilla into fourths. Place on a cookie sheet covered with a Silpat* and lightly spray each chip with water. Sprinkle with herbs or salt-free seasonings, if desired. Bake for 15 minutes. Turn chips over and lightly spray again with water. Bake another 10-15 minutes until crisp.

Chef's Note: You can also do this with whole wheat pita (but it would not be gluten-free).

*A Silpat is a non-stick, silicone baking mat. Nothing sticks to it and you can reuse. If you don't have one, you can use parchment paper.

CarriBEAN MANGO SALSA

Muy sabrosa!

INGREDIENTS:
2 cans low sodium black beans (rinsed and drained)
1 fresh mango, chopped
1/2 small red onion, finely diced
1 cucumber, peeled, seeded and chopped
1 red bell pepper, seeded and finely chopped
1 bunch cilantro leaves, chopped
1 bunch fresh mint, chopped (optional)
1 avocado, cubed (optional)
2 limes (juice and zest)
Splash of orange juice
Pinch of cumin

METHOD:
Mix all ingredients together. Chill. Serve in lettuce cups or avocado halves for a spectacular presentation.

Chef's Note: If mango is out of season, substitute canned pineapple chunks in their own juice.

EASY HUMMUS

A great way to eat more raw veggies.

INGREDIENTS:
1 x 15 ounce can salt-free garbanzo beans
Juice and zest from 1 lemon
2 Tablespoons tahini
2 cloves garlic (or more to taste)
Pinch of cumin

METHOD:
Drain beans, reserve liquid. In a food processor fitted with the "S" blade, process all ingredients until creamy and smooth, adding as much of the liquid as necessary to achieve the desired texture. Chill.

Variations: Add fresh herbs like cilantro or parsley, scallions, roasted red peppers or olives. Substitute roasted garlic for the fresh garlic.

Chef's Note: Substitute cannellini beans for the garbanzo beans.

HOLY MOLY BEAN DIP

As I always say, there is no recipe that can't be improved by the addition of garlic or chocolate. This recipe has both!

INGREDIENTS:
1 can low-sodium refried beans (black or pinto)
1 can salt-free beans (black or pinto)
1 cup salt-free salsa (such as Enrico's or Trader Joe's brand) or homemade Pico de Gallo (page 149)
1/3 cup fresh lime juice, including the zest (approximately 3 limes)
2 cloves garlic
1 Tablespoon chipotle paste (or 1/4 teaspoon chipotle powder)
2 teaspoons raw cacao powder
1/2 cup raw, shelled hemp seeds or raw cashews

METHOD:
Drain beans, reserving liquid. In a blender combine all ingredients except for the hemp seeds and blend until smooth and creamy, adding reserved bean liquid a little at a time if you need more liquid for processing. Add hemp seeds and blend again. Serve with baked, salt-free tortilla chips. Sprinkle with finely chopped green onions before serving.

Chef's Note: You can buy chipotle paste at www.chipotlepeople.com. You can also use canned chipotles in adobo sauce.

I CAN'T BELIEVE IT'S NOT TUNA PATE

(Raw)

Stuff this into endive leaves for a beautiful presentation.

INGREDIENTS:
1 cup raw almonds, soaked overnight
1 cup raw sunflower seeds, soaked overnight
Juice from 2-3 lemons
2 stalks celery, chopped
2 scallions, chopped
1/2 cup Italian parsley, chopped
2 Tablespoons kelp powder
1 Tablespoon dried dill
1 teaspoon dulse

METHOD:
Rinse the soaked nuts and seeds and place in food processor fitted with the "S" blade. Process with the lemon juice and only enough water to make it turn easily. Stir in the rest of the ingredients by hand. Chill. Delicious on flax crackers, in romaine leaves as a lettuce wrap, or in Nori rolls.

Chef's Note: I like to shape the pate into a fish with an olive for the eye and serve it over a bed of kale.

KALE or SPINACH DIP

This is also the filling I use in my lasagna.

INGREDIENTS:
1- box of extra firm water packed tofu (19 ounces each, I use Trader Joe's) **OR**
2 cans (15 ounce each) cannellini beans, drained and rinsed
2 ounces of fresh basil leaves
1 cups pine nuts, raw cashews or hemp seeds
2 cloves garlic (or more, to taste)
1/4 cup low-sodium miso
1/4 cup nutritional yeast
1/4 cup fresh lemon juice
1/8 teaspoon red pepper flakes (or more to taste)
2 pounds of frozen, chopped spinach (defrosted, drained with all of the liquid squeezed out) **OR** 1 pound frozen kale (defrosted, drained with all of the liquid squeezed out)

METHOD:
Place all ingredients except for the spinach or kale in a food processor fitted with the "S" blade and process until smooth and creamy. Add spinach or kale and process again until combined.

Chef's Note: Place in a hollowed-out, round loaf sourdough bread for a spectacular presentation.

PERFECT PESTO STUFFED MUSHROOMS

(Raw)

When Rip Esselstyn came to my home for dinner the first time, he ate the whole dozen by himself!

INGREDIENTS:
12 crimini mushrooms
1 cup pine nuts
2 cloves garlic
1 tablespoon yellow miso
1 cup fresh basil
Juice of one lemon, or to taste

METHOD:
Destem mushrooms and set aside. Remove some of the center if necessary. Place the rest of the ingredients in a food processor fitted with the "S" blade and process until smooth. Fill the mushroom cups and dehydrate 2-4 hours until warm.

Chef's Note: If you don't have a dehydrator, bake in a 350 degree F oven for 45 minutes or until soft.

SMOKEY CHIPOTLE CORN SALSA

This is my all-time favorite salsa.

INGREDIENTS:
1 x one pound bag frozen corn, defrosted
2 x 15 ounce cans pinto beans, drained and rinsed
1 pound of roma tomatoes (approximately 4), seeded and diced
1 bunch cilantro, chopped
4 scallions (or more, to taste), finely chopped
1 Tablespoon chipotle paste (or 1/4 teaspoon chipotle powder) or more to taste
Juice and zest from 4 limes
1 x 4 ounce can of black olives, rinsed and drained (optional)

METHOD:
Mix all ingredients together in a large bowl. Flavors will improve on sitting. Stir well before serving.

Chef's Note: This makes a great filling for a burrito. You can buy chipotle paste at www.chipotlepeople.com. You can also use canned chipotles in adobo sauce.

SWEET PEA GUACAMOLE

(Raw)

Much lower in fat and higher in fiber than traditional guacamole.

INGREDIENTS:
1 x 16 ounce bag of frozen peas, defrosted
3 firm roma tomatoes, diced
1 bunch of cilantro, chopped
1 jalapeño pepper, seeded and finely diced
1 shallot, finely diced
2 cloves garlic, minced
Juice of one lime, or more to taste
Pinch of cumin

METHOD: In a food processor fitted with the “S” blade, process peas until smooth. Transfer to a larger bowl. Stir in remaining ingredients by hand. Chill.

Chef’s Note: In a hurry? Buy a pound of store-bought, ready-made guacamole. Place in a food processor fitted with the “S” blade and add a one pound bag of frozen, defrosted peas. Process until smooth.

POWer PATE

(Raw)

*A tasty appetizer spread made from **P**eas, **O**nions and **W**alnuts.*
Recipe by Michelle Wolf,
with inspiration from her mother Pauline.
Michelle says it's always a crowd pleaser
when her mom serves it to guests.

INGREDIENTS:
2 packages frozen peas (defrosted)
2 large Spanish yellow onions (chopped)
1-1/2 cups ground walnuts

METHOD:
Mash peas with a fork or blend in a food processor. Sauté onions in water or low-sodium vegetable broth. Mix all ingredients together in a large bowl. Season to taste with Mrs. Dash or a similar salt-free seasoning like Benson's Table Tasty.

Chef's Note: Great served on cucumber rounds.

BEVERAGES

ALMOND MILK

(Raw)

Why buy plant milk in a box laden with sodium when you can make your own for just pennies a glass?

INGREDIENTS:
1 cup raw almonds (or your favorite nut or seed)

METHOD:
Soak the almonds overnight in filtered water. Be sure to cover completely as they expand as they absorb water. In the morning, drain completely and rinse well several times. Place the almonds in a blender with 3 cups of filtered water. Blend on high speed until the almonds are fully incorporated into the liquid. Pour mixture into a paint straining bag (that is new and has not been used for painting!). You can get these at any hardware store for about 99 cents. Strain the milk from the pulp over a bowl until you can't squeeze any more liquid out of the pulp. You can reserve the pulp for another use such as making cookies or crackers. Refrigerate any unused milk. Last about 2-3 days. If you like your nut milk thicker and richer, more like cream, just add less water. For thinner almond milk, add more water.

CHEAP & EASY METHOD:
Place 1 Tablespoon raw almond butter in a blender with 3 cups filtered water and blend until smooth.

Chef's Note: For sweet almond milk, add 12 deglet noor dates, 1 Tablespoon alcohol-free vanilla and a capful of almond extract.

APPLE PIE SMOOTHIE

(Raw)

Taste like apple pie in a glass!

INGREDIENTS:
12 ounces almond milk
2 cups frozen peaches
1/2 cup unsweetened apple butter
1 banana, frozen
Dates, to taste
1 Tablespoon alcohol-free vanilla extract
1 teaspoon cinnamon
1/4 teaspoon nutmeg
Ice cubes

METHOD:
Place all ingredients in blender and blend until smooth.

Chef's Note: If you can't find apple butter, try substituting unsweetened apple juice for all or part of the almond milk.

BASIC VANILLA SHAKE

(Raw)

Serve in a milkshake glass for a classic vanilla shake.

INGREDIENTS:
8 ounces almond milk
1 banana, frozen
Dates, to taste
1 Tablespoon alcohol-free vanilla extract
1/2 teaspoon almond extract (optional)
Ice cubes

METHOD:
Place all ingredients in blender and process until smooth.

Chef's Note: Add raw cacao nibs for a Cookies & Cream Shake.

CARAMEL FAKIATTO

The small amount of caramel extract really gives this rich, creamy treat that "je ne sais quoi".

INGREDIENTS:
8 ounces unsweetened chocolate almond milk
2 Tablespoons raw cacao powder
1 large frozen banana
Dates, to taste
12 ice cubes (or more to reach desired thickness)
1/2 teaspoon caramel extract

METHOD:
Place all ingredients in a high-powered blender and blend until thick and smooth.
Don't share!

Chef's Note: You don't have to use raw cacao in any of these recipes. Just be sure if you use cocoa powder it's a great tasting high quality alkali-free brand.

CHOCOLATE COVERED CHERRY SMOOTHIE

The pretty shade of pink reminds me of a cherry cordial.

INGREDIENTS:
12 ounces unsweetened chocolate almond milk
2 Tablespoons unsweetened cherry butter
2 cups frozen cherries
1 banana, frozen
Dates, to taste
2 Tablespoons raw cacao powder
1 - 2 Tablespoons raw cacao nibs
Ice cubes

METHOD:
Place all ingredients except for cacao nibs in blender and blend until smooth. Add nibs and pulse briefly.

HOMEMADE PISTACHIO MILK
(Raw)

INGREDIENTS:
2 cups raw pistachios

METHOD:
Soak nuts in water for several hours. Drain and rinse well. Place in blender with 2 cups of water (more for a thinner, less rich milk) and blend on high. Pour through a strainer bag and gently squeeze, separating pulp from milk.

THE INCREDIBLE HULK
(Raw)
I love the vibrant green color of this juice.

INGREDIENTS:
1 head of kale
1 cucumber
2 apples
Juice of one lime

METHOD:
Place all ingredients in a juicer. Citrus fruits must be either peeled first or squeezed separately. Enjoy immediately.

Chef's Note: I prefer green smoothies to juice because then you also have the healthy pulp and fiber. My friend, Andy Greene, actually makes this juice in her blender and she says it tastes great!

IT'S EASY BEING GREEN SMOOTHIE

(Raw)

I have this for breakfast almost every day and never tire of it.

INGREDIENTS:
16 ounces fresh squeezed orange juice (or 2-3 fresh oranges)
1 bunch kale (approximately 12 ounces)
2 frozen, ripe bananas
2 cups frozen mango
Fresh mint leaves to taste (optional)

METHOD:
In a blender, blend orange juice (or oranges) with kale until smooth. Add frozen fruit and blend until completely blended and thick.

Chef's Note:
For a Creamsicle effect, use half unsweetened almond milk and half orange juice. You can also use spinach instead of kale.

MINT CHOCOLATE CHIP SMOOTHIE

(Raw)

Looks and tastes like mint chocolate chip ice cream!

INGREDIENTS:
8 ounces pistachio milk
1 banana, frozen
Dates, to taste
1 Tablespoon alcohol-free vanilla extract
20 fresh mint leaves (more or less, to taste)
3 large kale leaves
Ice cubes
Handful of raw cacao nibs

METHOD:
Place all ingredients in blender except for the nibs and process until smooth. Add raw cacao nibs and blend briefly.

NUTRIENT RICH CHOCOLATE SMOOTHIE

(Raw)

No one will know there are any greens in this smoothie unless you tell them.

INGREDIENTS:
6 ounces unsweetened chocolate almond milk
4 ounces pomegranate juice
6 ounces organic baby spinach
1 banana, frozen
Dates, to taste
3 Tablespoons raw cacao powder or carob powder
2 cups frozen blueberries
1 Tablespoon flax seeds

METHOD:
Place all ingredients in blender and process until smooth.

Chef's Note: This smoothie is also delicious without the dates and cacao powder.

PUMPKIN PIE SMOOTHIE

Tastes like pumpkin pie in a glass.

INGREDIENTS:
16 ounces unsweetened almond milk
2 bananas
Dates, to taste
1 Tablespoon alcohol-free vanilla extract
1 x 14 ounce can pumpkin (not pie filling)
1 Tablespoon pumpkin pie spice
Ice cubes

METHOD: Place all ingredients in a blender and blend until smooth.

ENTICING ENTREES

CHEF AJ'S DISAPPEARING LASAGNA

People always ask me how well this freezes. I honestly don't know as there have never been any leftovers!

INGREDIENTS:
2 boxes of no boil rice lasagna noodles (De Boles)
6 cups of your favorite no-oil marinara sauce
1- box extra firm water-packed tofu (19 ounces each, I use Trader Joe's) **OR**
2 cans (15 ounce each) cannellini beans, drained and rinsed
2 ounces fresh basil leaves
1 cup pine nuts, raw cashews or hemp seeds
2 cloves garlic (or more, to taste)
1/4 cup low-sodium miso
1/4 cup nutritional yeast
1/4 cup fresh lemon juice
1/8 teaspoon red pepper flakes (or more to taste)
1 x 4-ounce can sliced olives, rinsed and drained (optional)
2 pounds frozen, chopped spinach (defrosted, drained with all of the liquid squeezed out) **OR** 1 pound frozen kale (defrosted, drained with all of the liquid squeezed out)
2 pounds sliced mushrooms (I like to use crimini or baby bellas)
1/4 cup low sodium tamari
1 large red onion, finely diced
Faux parmesan (see page 142)

METHOD:
Make the filling in a food processor fitted with the "S" blade by adding one box of tofu or 2 cans of beans, 2 ounces basil, 2 cloves garlic, 1/4 cup each lemon juice, miso and nutritional yeast. 1 cup of the pine nuts and 1/8 of a teaspoon of red pepper flakes. Puree until smooth. Add drained spinach or kale and process again.
In a large non-stick sauté pan, sauté the onion in 2 Tablespoons water until translucent, about 8 minutes, adding more water if necessary. Add garlic, mushrooms and tamari and sauté until browned. Taste mixture, adding chopped garlic and more tamari according to your taste. Cook until mushrooms appear to be glazed and there is no more liquid left in the pan.

Pour 3 cups of the sauce into a lasagna pan or 9 x 13 inch pan. Place one layer of the no cook noodles on top. Cover the noodles with half of the tofu/spinach mixture, then with half of the mushroom mixture. Place another layer of noodles on the mushroom mixture and add the remaining half of the tofu/spinach mixture and the remaining half of the mushroom mixture. Place one more layer of noodles on top of the mushroom mixture and smother evenly with the remaining 3 cups of sauce. Sprinkle the sliced olives on top of the sauce along with a liberal sprinkling of faux parmesan. Bake uncovered in a preheated 375 degree F oven for an hour.
Let set 10 minutes before slicing.

Chef's Note: If you have time, marinate the sliced mushrooms in the tamari several hours in advance or even the night before. Make sure the top layer of noodles are fully covered with sauce.

HEARTY LENTIL LOAF

No soy or bread crumbs in this loaf, just whole food goodness.

INGREDIENTS:
1 box cooked lentils (available at Trader Joe's) or 3 cups cooked lentils
1 x 16 ounce bag of frozen carrots, defrosted and drained
2 cups red onion (about 1 large)
2 cloves garlic, peeled
2 cups raw walnuts, divided
2 cups uncooked oats (not instant), divided
1/2 cup chopped Italian parsley, finely chopped
2 Tablespoons sundried tomato powder

METHOD:
Preheat oven to 350 degrees F. Combine lentils, carrots, onion, parsley, one cup of the walnuts and one cup of the oats in a food processor fitted with the "S" blade. Process ingredients until smooth and almost paste-like. Place mixture in a bowl and then stir in the second cup of oats and the second cup of chopped walnuts. Stir in the seasonings. Pour mixture into a silicone standard loaf pan and bake uncovered for 50-55 minutes until golden brown. Remove from oven and let sit at least 10 minutes before inverting onto a serving dish. Invert and let cool another 5 minutes and then slice. Delicious, even without any sauce or gravy of any kind, or add your favorite condiments such as ketchup, mustard or BBQ Sauce. Stuff cold leftovers into pita pockets for a great lunch!

Chef's Note: I like to make this in a silicone bundt pan and fill it with Cranberry Relish (page 140).

I split it into 2 loaf pans. We weren't crazy about it - it was too much for my processor & the walnuts I added unprocessed should have been broken down more. I love all the ingredients - would maybe make in a casserole next time - shaping into a loaf

KUNG PAO TOFU

INGREDIENTS:
1 pound extra firm tofu cut into 1/2 inch cubes*
1 cup unsalted peanuts
1 cup low sodium tamari
1 cup mirin
1/2 cup dry sherry
3 Tablespoons arrowroot
6 cloves garlic
Red pepper flakes or chili paste, to taste
Chopped scallions, for garnish

serve over brown rice noodles?

METHOD:
Mix all ingredients except tofu, scallions and peanuts in a saucepan. Heat until thickened and keep warm. Add sauce to cooked tofu and stir until well coated. Garnish with peanuts and scallions.

*To cook tofu cubes, mix equal amounts of low sodium tamari and rice vinegar. Add a few tablespoons to a non-stick pan and coat the tofu evenly. Cook until tofu cubes are golden brown on all sides.

Chef's Note: Mirin is a sweet Japanese rice wine.

I thawed frozen broccoli to add to leftovers

Marc, Dad & I liked

Needs a starch to go with heavy amount of sauce. Made soba noodles but also try rice next time in addition to noodles since Marc liked noodles.

Also steam veggies could be nice mixed in.

The peanuts are a nice addition & next time add most of the whole bunch of green onion

LENTIL TACOS

One of my students, Karen Spector, brought this to a potluck and it was a huge hit. Karen won an award at her work for being the "green smoothie queen."

INGREDIENTS:
1 cup chopped onion
1 garlic clove, minced
1 cup dry lentils, rinsed
1 Tablespoon chili powder
2 teaspoons ground cumin
1 teaspoon oregano
14 ounces water
1 cup salt-free salsa
Salt-free seasoning, to taste

METHOD:
Put everything in the crock pot and cook on high for 8-12 hours, stirring occasionally and adding water as needed. This taco filling can be used anywhere you would normally use a meat taco filling, such as in taco shells and on salads.

Chef's Note: You can buy a slow cooker now for under 20 bucks. It is a great investment and I guarantee you *will* use it. You can put up a quick soup or stew in the morning and have a hot, healthy dinner ready for you when you come home.

next time either cook on low whole time or switch to low sooner. Try to avoid adding any extra water if possible to maintain flavor.
Served w/ ~~sour~~ leftover schmear or vegan mayo or simply avoca[do] tomatoes & onions. Warmed soft tort.

Filling & tasty. Make again - maybe serve w/ frit[os] or corn

MELANZANA ABBODANZA

Which translated means "Eggplant Abundance."

INGREDIENTS:
1 recipe of Chef AJ's Disappearing Lasagna (page 100) minus the rice lasagna noodles
1-2 eggplants (depending on size)

METHOD:
Preheat oven to 400. Slice eggplant (with skin on) into 1/4" slices and place on Silipat or non-stick pan. Sprinkle with your favorite salt-free seasoning and bake for 20 minutes. Turn slices over and bake for an additional 20 minutes or until eggplant begins to shrink and soften. Follow the directions for the lasagna but use the eggplant slices in place of the noodles.

MEXICAN LASAGNA

This is one of the first recipes I made up when I was a teenager.

INGREDIENTS:
2 boxes brown rice lasagna noodles
4 cans oil-free low sodium refried pinto beans
6 cups salt-free salsa (Enrico's or Trader Joe's) or homemade Pico de Gallo (page 149)
2 x 16 ounce bags frozen corn, defrosted
Chopped scallions and olives for garnish (optional)

METHOD:
Preheat oven to 350. In a large bowl, mix the beans and corn together. Place 3 cups of the salsa on the bottom of a 9 x 13 inch pan. Place one layer of noodles over the salsa and spoon half of the bean and corn mixture over the noodles. Place another layer of noodles on the corn and bean mixture and then place the remaining corn and bean mixture over the noodles. Place a third layer of noodles on top of the corn and bean mixture and the remaining 3 cups of salsa over the top layer of noodles. Make sure the top layer of noodles are completely covered with salsa. Bake uncovered for 30 minutes or until heated through. Let set 10 minutes before slicing. Garnish with chopped scallions and olives, if desired.

Chef's Note: This is great with a dollop of Sweet Pea Guacamole on top.

NOT SO SLOPPY JOES

INGREDIENTS:
2 cups red onion, diced (one large)
2 cups red bell pepper, diced (one large)
2 cloves garlic, pressed
1 can diced salt-free tomatoes (14.5 ounces)
1 can salt-free tomato paste (6 ounces)
1 teaspoon chili powder
2 Tablespoon sun-dried tomato powder
2 x 15 ounce cans salt-free black beans, drained
1 lime, juiced

METHOD:
In a non-stick pan, water sauté onions, peppers and garlic for 7-8 minutes until soft and translucent. Add diced tomatoes, tomato paste, sun dried tomato powder and beans. Stir until well combined and cook for another 2-3 minutes until heated. Remove from heat and stir in lime juice.

Chef's Note: Great served over a bed of steamed kale.

PORTABELLA MUSHROOM STROGANOFF

INGREDIENTS: (Sauce)
1 box Mori Nu Silken Tofu (12.4 ounces)
1/2 cup water
3 Tablespoons fresh lemon juice (include zest from the lemon)
3 Tablespoons low sodium tamari
2 Tablespoons tahini
2 cloves garlic
1 inch piece of ginger (more or less, to taste)

METHOD:
Place all ingredients in blender and blend until smooth.

INGREDIENTS: (Filling)
1 red onion, minced
1 pound portabella mushrooms, sliced
1 teaspoon oregano
Chopped Italian parsley, for garnish

METHOD:
Water sauté onion until translucent. Add mushrooms and sauté until they become limp and moisture has evaporated. Stir in oregano. Pour sauce over and mix well. Garnish with fresh parsley.

Chef's Note: This is great served over brown rice.

QUICK SUN DRIED TOMATO MARINARA

(Raw)

This sauce takes minutes to make but tastes like it was slow simmered for hours. The best part is, there are no pots to clean or vegetables to cut up.

INGREDIENTS:
1 cup oil-free sun dried tomatoes, soaked in water
3-4 fresh Roma tomatoes (approximately 12 ounces)
1 red bell pepper, seeded (approximately 8 ounces)
1-2 cloves garlic, peeled
3-4 pitted dates
1 shallot (approximately 1 ounce) or red onion equivalent
1 Tablespoon sun-dried tomato powder
3-4 fresh basil leaves

METHOD:
In a blender, blend all ingredients until smooth. If you prefer a chunkier consistency, use a food processor fitted with the "S" blade and process all ingredients until desired consistency is reached. Serve over your favorite healthy noodles such as those made from rice, tofu, sea vegetables or zucchini. To make zucchini noodles, peel zucchini and then make noodles using a Spiralizer, Saladacco or vegetable peeler.

Chef's Note: If you have a high-powered blender, you can make this sauce hot right in the blender.

STIRRED, NOT FRIED
(Raw)

INGREDIENTS:
Your favorite veggies, cut up in small pieces. I like to use broccoli, bok choy, pea pods, carrots, peas, corn, red pepper, red onion, bean sprouts and cilantro.
Sauce:
1 cup raw almond butter
1 ripe avocado
1/3 cup lime juice (about 3), including zest
3 Tablespoons low sodium tamari
4-6 cloves garlic
2 inch piece of ginger
1 teaspoon tamarind paste
6 dates
10-20 mint leaves
Red pepper flakes, to taste (optional)
1/2 cup water (or water from a Thai young coconut)
Chopped almonds and bean sprouts for garnish (optional)

METHOD:
Place all ingredients in a blender and blend until smooth, adding only enough water to allow the blender to process. Pour over vegetables and coat well. Top with beans sprouts, chopped almonds and more cilantro, if desired.

Chef's Note: Even better the next day after the flavors have a chance to marinate.

STUFFED BUTTERNUT SQUASH

This has been my favorite fall entrée since I was 7 years old.

INGREDIENTS:
3-4 butternut squash (depending on their size)
Grain of choice (brown rice, stuffing, quinoa)
1 pound Sunshine Burgers (breakfast flavor)
1 red onion
2 cups chopped celery
2 cups chopped mushrooms
1 cup chopped fresh Italian parsley

METHOD:
Preheat oven to 400 degrees F. Cut squash in half and bake, cut side down, on a Silpat (or non-stick pan) approximately 40 minutes, until soft. Remove seeds. Scoop out squash, leaving a 1/4" border, and place in a large bowl. Prepare grain of choice according to package directions. In a large pan, water sauté onion, celery and mushrooms until soft, about 10 minutes. Add sausage substitute and sauté until browned. Add to squash and mix well. Stir in parsley. Add desired amount of grain to squash mixture. Fill squash halves with the stuffing mixture. Bake for another 30 minutes until browned.

Chef's Note: Sometimes I add dried unsweetened cranberries and pecans to the stuffing. Sunshine Burgers are a whole food frozen veggie burger (www.sunshineburger.com).

SWEET POTATO NACHOS

When you're vegan, not many people invite you over for dinner. And when you are a chef, even fewer do. My friend, Margaret Rudoy, dared to have me over and created this delicious dish that is now a staple in our home.

INGREDIENTS:
Sweet potatoes (one per person)

METHOD:
Preheat oven to 450 degrees F. Cut sweet potato into uniform slices, approximately 1/4". Place on Silpat or non-stick baking sheet and sprinkle with smoked paprika. Bake for 20 minutes, flip over and bake for another 10-15 minutes until done. These are "the chip" part of your nachos.

ASSEMBLY:
Place several sweet potato "chips" on a plate and fully load them with oil-free refried beans, chopped tomato, corn, cilantro, onion, olives, jalepeno peppers or anything you would normally enjoy on your nachos.

Chef's Note: I like to create a "nacho bar" and let guests build their own nachos. If you use organic sweet potatoes, there is no need to peel. Lots of fiber and nutrients in the skin.

SWEET POTATO AND BLUE CORN ENCHILADAS

INGREDIENTS: (Sauce)
1 red onion, chopped
2 cloves garlic, crushed
1 - 28 ounce can salt-free tomatoes
3 Tablespoons chili powder
1 teaspoon cumin
3 Tablespoons arrowroot powder
1 Tablespoon low sodium tamari
1 and 1/2 cups water

METHOD: (Sauce)
Place the onion, garlic and liquid in a pot and cook 8-10 minutes until soft. Stir in tomato and spices and cook on low heat for 15 minutes. Add tamari and arrowroot powder and stir until thickened.

INGREDIENTS: (Filling)
2 cups Pico de Gallo (page 149) or store-bought, salt-free salsa
3 cups sweet potatoes
1 pound bag frozen roasted corn, defrosted
12 blue corn tortillas
Topping: sliced olives and scallions (optional)

METHOD: (Filling)
Peel sweet potatoes and boil, steam or microwave until soft. Mash. Stir in remainder of ingredients.

ASSEMBLY:
Preheat oven to 350 degrees F. Cover the bottom of the baking dish with half of the enchilada sauce. Spread sweet potato filling down the center of each tortilla. Roll up and place seam side down in the dish. Pour the remaining sauce over the tortillas and sprinkle sliced olives, if using, over the top. Bake for 30 minutes. Sprinkle with scallions and top with Sweet Pea Guacamole (page 86) if desired.

SWEET AND SOUR TEMPEH

INGREDIENTS:
1 pound tempeh
1 and 1/2 cups unsweetened pineapple juice
1/2 cup unsweetened ketchup
1/2 cup date syrup
1/4 cup unsweetened brown rice vinegar
3 Tablespoons arrowroot powder
1 clove garlic (or more to taste)
1 inch piece of ginger (or more to taste)
1 green pepper, cut into squares

METHOD:
Cut tempeh into triangles. Combine all ingredients in a saucepan except for the tempeh and the green pepper. Heat and stir until boiling. Reduce heat and simmer until thickened. Keep warm. Add tempeh to a hot wok or non-stick skillet and water sauté until browned. Add sauce and green pepper and cook briefly until hot.

SALADS & DRESSINGS

ARTICHOKE BRAZIL NUT DRESSING

This recipe was inspired by Zel Allen, author of "The Nut Gourmet" and publisher of www.vegparadise.com.

INGREDIENTS:
1/2 cup raw Brazil nuts
1 x 14-ounce can water-packed artichoke hearts, rinsed and drained
1 cup unsweetened almond milk
1/4 cup fresh lemon juice
1/4 cup rice vinegar
4 Tablespoons nutritional yeast
1 teaspoon salt-free seasoning (or more to taste)

METHOD:
Grind the Brazil nuts in your blender or in a coffee grinder. Place remaining ingredients in the blender along with the nuts and blend until smooth and creamy.

Chef's Note: Nutritional yeast, high in B vitamins, is different than brewer's yeast. It is often found in the bulk section or supplement section.

AUNT MELONY'S
CAESAR SALAD DRESSING

Melony Jorenson was the most recent winner of the "Unprocessed Challenge". She created this delicious, creamy nut-free dressing.

INGREDIENTS:
2 cups water
1x15-ounce can cannellini beans, drained and rinsed
3 cloves garlic
3/4 cup lemon juice
4 Tablespoons low sodium miso
6 Tablespoons nutritional yeast
1 Tablespoon rice vinegar
1/2 teaspoon xanthan gum

METHOD:
Place all ingredients in blender and blend until smooth. Add xanthan gum and blend again briefly.

Chef's Note: This dressing is delicious on baked potatoes and steamed veggies.

CUCUMBER PEANUT SALAD

INGREDIENTS:
3 large cucumbers – peeled, seeded and chopped (about 2 pounds)
Juice and zest of 2 limes
Red pepper flakes, to taste
Chopped fresh mint
1/2 cup chopped roasted unsalted peanuts

METHOD:
Mix all ingredients except for the peanuts and mix well. Let flavors meld at least 30 minutes before serving. Add chopped peanuts right before serving.

Chef's Note: You can substitute fresh basil or cilantro for the mint.

FENNEL SALAD

(Raw)

One of my Kitchen Angels, Ellen Greek, brought this to a potluck. Hard to believe that something with only 3 ingredients could be so delicious.

INGREDIENTS:
2 bulbs of fennel
1 lemon
20 dates

METHOD:
Slice the fennel very thin into a bowl. Keep the green top to decorate the salad. Slice the dates and mixed them with the fennel. Pour the lemon juice over this and mix it well.

Chef's Note: You can serve this cold or room temperature.

GINGER SLAW

(Raw)

INGREDIENTS:
Slaw:
2 cups shredded carrots
2 cups shredded purple cabbage
2 cups jicama (cut into long thin strips)
Cilantro and pumpkin seeds for garnish (optional)

Dressing:
1/2 cup orange juice
Juice of one lime, plus zest
1/2 ounce fresh ginger, pressed

METHOD:
Combine vegetables in large bowl. Whisk dressing ingredients together and pour over vegetables. Garnish with cilantro and/or pumpkin seeds if desired.

GREEN GOODNESS DRESSING

(Raw)

If you use only the green parts, the dressing will be really bright green like Green Goddess.

INGREDIENTS:
2 cups filtered water
1 cup fresh lemon juice
2/3 cup sesame seeds
1/3 cup low-sodium miso paste
2 cloves garlic
1/2 ounce fresh ginger
8 deglet noor dates (or to taste)
1/2 bunch of scallions (about 3 ounces)
1/4 - 1/2 teaspoon xanthan gum (to thicken)

METHOD:
Place all ingredients except for the thickener in a high-powered blender and process until smooth. Adjust for taste. Add xanthan gum and blend again briefly. Keep refrigerated.

HAIL TO THE KALE SALAD

(Raw)

Even people who say they don't like kale will gobble this up.

INGREDIENTS:

Salad:
2 large heads of curly kale (about 24 ounces)
Chopped almonds

Dressing:
1 cup raw almond butter (unsweetened and unsalted)
1 cup coconut water (or regular water)
1/4 cup fresh lime juice (about 2) and zest
2 cloves garlic
Fresh, peeled ginger (approximately 1" or 1/2 of an ounce)
2 Tablespoons low sodium tamari
4 pitted dates (soaked in water if not soft)
1/2 teaspoon red pepper flakes

METHOD:
In a high-powered blender, combine all dressing ingredients and blend until smooth and creamy. Remove the thick, larger stems from the kale. Place the kale leaves in a large bowl. Pour 2 cups of the dressing over the kale and, using an Ulu blade, massage the dressing into the kale while finely chopping the kale. Sprinkle with seeds or nuts before serving, if desired. Like a woman, this only gets better with age. Refrigerate any unused dressing.

Chef's Note: This salad is also delicious when peanut butter, shredded raw beets and carrots are added. If you have a dehydrator, dip kale leaves in the dressing and dehydrate for delicious kale chips! If you are allergic to nuts, use tahini (sesame seed paste) or sunflower seed butter in place of the nut butter.

HEMP SEED LIME DRESSING

(Raw)

INGREDIENTS:
1/2 cup hemp seeds
1/2 cup lime juice plus zest
1 and 1/2 cups water
1" piece fresh ginger (or more, to taste)
2 cloves garlic (or more, to taste)
4 whole pitted dates (or more, to taste)
1 Tablespoon salt-free seasoning
1/2 teaspoon xanthan gum

METHOD:
Place all ingredients except for the xanthan gum in a blender and blend until smooth and creamy. Taste and adjust, if necessary. Add xanthan gum and briefly blend again.

Chef's Note: If you can't find hemp seeds, substitute soaked cashews.

HUMMUS DRESSING

INGREDIENTS:
1 cup hummus (page 80)
3 Tablespoons fresh lemon juice
3 Tablespoons fresh lime juice
3 Tablespoons orange juice
1 Tablespoon salt-free stone-ground mustard
3 soft, pitted dates
1 clove garlic (or more to taste)
1/2" piece of fresh ginger (or more to taste)
1/2 cup raw cashews

METHOD:
Place all ingredients except cashews in blender and blend until smooth. Add cashews and blend again until thick and creamy. Refrigerate any unused dressing.

NOSTADA SALAD

We serve this at the Challenge dinners to show people how you can make a hot, healthy, delicious meal in no time. When they taste it, they begin to realize you don't need oil to enjoy a delicious salad.

INGREDIENTS:
Romaine lettuce, chopped
Chopped tomatoes
Chopped scallions
Chopped cilantro
Oil-free refried beans, warmed
Frozen corn, warmed
Fresh lime juice
Olives and pumpkin seeds for garnish (optional)

METHOD:
Place lettuce in a large bowl. Add a big scoop of warmed corn and beans. Top with tomatoes, cilantro and olives and pumpkin seeds, if desired. Squeeze lime juice over the top and enjoy immediately.

Chef's Note: Also good with Pico de Gallo (page 149) and Sweet Pea Guacamole (page 86).

ORANGE SESAME DRESSING

(Raw)

I made this up during a class to show how easy it is to "just throw stuff in a blender" and make a delicious dressing.

INGREDIENTS:
3-4 oranges (without the peel)
1/2 cup unhulled sesame seeds
1/8 cup low-sodium miso paste

METHOD:
Place all ingredients in a blender and blend until smooth.

Chef's Note: This is especially delicious on chopped kale.

SPINACH WALDORF

(Raw)

I served this beautiful dish to Chef Brian Malarkey on "Kick-Off Cookoff".

INGREDIENTS:
1 batch Hail To The Kale dressing (page 122)
Spinach
Thinly sliced red apples
Shredded beets
Shredded carrots
Chopped walnuts
Pomegranate seeds

METHOD:
Place spinach, apples, carrots and beets in a large bowl and toss with "Hail To The Kale" dressing. Sprinkle walnuts and pomegranate seeds on top before serving.

Chef's Note: Trader Joes sells frozen pomegranate seeds. I stock up on them so I can have them all year round, even when pomegranates are not in season.

SAVORY SOUPS

CREAM OF ZUCCHINI SOUP

(Raw)

Start eating this soup made from zucchini
and soon you'll fit into your bikini!

INGREDIENTS:
1 and 1/2 pounds zucchini, cut up (about 3)
12 ounces unsweetened hemp milk
1 clove garlic (or more, taste)
3 Tablespoons fresh lemon juice
4 large basil leaves
4 pitted dates
½ cup hemp seeds
1 Tablespoon sundried tomato powder

METHOD:
In a blender, combine all ingredients until smooth. Garnish with small cubes of zucchini or sprouts, if desired. Enjoy immediately. Delicious served warm or cold.

Chef Notes: If you can't find hemp milk, unsweetened almond milk works great.

CREAMY CORN CHOWDER

(Raw)

I prefer this soup served cold like a gazpacho.

INGREDIENTS:
2 and 1/2 cups almond milk
2 and 1/2 cups corn kernels
1 small shallot
1 avocado

METHOD:
Puree all ingredients in a blender until smooth. Ladle into bowls and sprinkle with cilantro leaves, diced avocado and corn kernels.

Chef's Note: You can defrost frozen corn or use fresh for this super easy soup. It's also great with a little sun-dried tomato powder or chipotle powder.

DREAM OF TOMATO SOUP

(Raw)

A much healthier version of a childhood favorite with a twist. Reminiscent of Campbell's Cream of Tomato Soup

INGREDIENTS:
1 pound Roma tomatoes, chopped
2 red bell peppers, seeded
1 clove garlic
6-8 large basil leaves
Juice of 1 lemon
2 Tablespoons sun-dried tomato powder* (or more, to taste)
1/4 teaspoon chipotle powder (or more, to taste)
1 cup shelled hemp seeds (optional)

METHOD:
Place all ingredients except for hemp seeds in a high-powered blender and blend until smooth. By using a high-powered blender, the soup will become warm without having to heat it. Add hemp seeds and blend again until creamy.

*If you can't find sun-dried tomato powder, you can easily make your own by taking the hard sun-dried tomatoes (not oil packed) and grinding them in a coffee grinder.

Chef's Note: This is also delicious over pasta or steamed veggies.

EASY EDAMAME SOUP

With tofu, miso and edamame,
this soup has triple the soy power!

INGREDIENTS:
12 cups water (or low sodium vegetable stock)
4 cups broccoli florets
4 cups edamame
1 pound tofu (cut into cubes)
2 bunches of scallions
6 Tablespoons low sodium miso
2 cloves garlic (or more to taste)
1 x 2" piece of ginger

METHOD:
Bring water (or stock) to a boil. Add tofu and vegetables and return to a boil. Simmer for 4-5 minutes until vegetables are bright green and crisp. Place garlic and ginger through a garlic press and add to soup. Dissolve miso separately in 1 cup of the soup water, then blend into soup.

GARDEN GAZPACHO

(Raw)

This reminds me of my favorite gazpacho from Café Marmalade.

INGREDIENTS:
2 carrots
1 yellow bell pepper
1 cucumber, peeled and seeded
1/2 red onion
8 Roma tomatoes
2 cloves garlic
Juice of 2 limes
1/2 cup chopped cilantro
1/4 cup chopped Italian parsley
Pinch of cumin
Pinch of cayenne pepper
Avocado cubes for garnish (optional)

METHOD:
In a food processor fitted with the "S" blade, process each vegetable separately until desired size is reached. I like to vary the texture so I will chop the carrots very fine and make the other vegetables larger by increments. If you prefer your soup less chunky, you can juice the tomatoes separately through a juicer. Mix all ingredients together in a bowl and chill for at least 4 hours. Season to taste and garnish each serving with cubes of avocado, if desired.

Chef's Note: I like to add chipotle powder to mine to make it hotter.

NUTRIENT RICH BLACK BEAN SOUP

No one will guess that there are two pounds of greens hidden in this delicious soup.

INGREDIENTS:
12 cups low sodium vegetable broth or water
6 cans salt-free black beans
2 red onions, peeled
8 cloves garlic, peeled
1 pound crimini mushrooms
1 pound baby bok choy (approximately 3)
1 pound chopped greens (kale, collard, mustard, chard or a combination)
2 large sweet potatoes, peeled if not organic
2 bags frozen corn, defrosted (16 ounces each)
2 Tablespoons sundried tomato powder (or more, to taste)
2 Tablespoons cumin and 2 Tablespoons oregano
1 Tablespoon chipotle paste (or 1/4 teaspoon powder) or more, to taste
Juice and zest of 4 limes

METHOD:
Place water or broth in a large soup pot and bring to a boil. Reduce heat and add beans, one pound of the corn, garlic, onions, sweet potatoes and greens in a large soup pot. Simmer uncovered for 30 minutes. There is no need to cut anything up as the soup will be blended. If you are using salt-free beans, it is not even necessary to rinse or drain them. Remove from heat and blend soup with an immersion blender. Stir in cumin, oregano, chipotle paste, sundried tomato powder, lime juice and second bag of corn. Garnish with pepitas and cilantro, if desired.

Chef's Note: For more texture, you can also leave half of the beans (3 cans) whole and stir them in after the soup is blended.

POPEYE'S PERFECTION

(Raw)

INGREDIENTS:
10 ounces filtered water or unsweetened almond milk
1 Tablespoon sundried tomato powder
12 ounces baby organic spinach
1 small shallot
1 cup ripe avocado
2 Tablespoons fresh lemon juice
1 large date, soaked (or more, to taste)
Hemp seeds for garnish (optional)

METHOD:
Place water and tomato powder in a blender and blend until dissolved. Add spinach, shallot, and date and blend until smooth. Add avocado and lemon and blend briefly until smooth. Do not over process the avocado. Sprinkle with hemp seeds, if desired. Enjoy immediately.

STOMPIN' AT THE SAVOY CABBAGE SOUP

This delicious soup is a healthier version of the sweet and sour cabbage soup my Russian grandmother would make on Friday nights. It's so good that it would even make Louis Armstrong stomp!

INGREDIENTS:
2 large yellow onions, diced (about 4 cups)
1 cup carrots, sliced (about 6 carrots)
1 cup celery, diced (about 8 stalks)
1 pound crimini mushrooms, sliced
6 cloves garlic, peeled and pressed
8 cups water
2 cans (14.5 ounces each) salt-free diced tomatoes
1 can (6 ounces) salt-free tomato paste
1 head savoy cabbage, shredded (about 10 cups)
1 cup fresh basil, chiffonade (ribbon slices)
1 Tablespoon sundried tomato powder
4 Tablespoons spicy pecan vinegar

METHOD:
Water sauté onions until translucent and soft, about 8-10 minutes. Add carrots, celery, garlic and mushrooms and sauté another 8-10 minutes until carrots are soft. Add water, diced tomatoes and tomato paste and bring to a boil. Stir in sundried tomato powder. Add shredded cabbage and reduce heat. Cook for a few more minutes until cabbage becomes slightly softened. I only cook it 2-3 more minutes because I like my cabbage to still have a slight crunch, but you can cook it longer if you prefer. Remove from heat and stir in basil and vinegar. Serve.

Chef's Note: Savoy cabbage is a very pretty cabbage available at most supermarkets. If you can't find it, feel free to substitute Napa cabbage, regular cabbage, or even kale. Spicy pecan vinegar is made by Cuisine Perel. You could also use apple cider vinegar.

SWEET POTATO SOUP WITH CANNELINI BEANS AND RAINBOW CHARD

You can also make this soup with butternut squash or white potatoes in place of the sweet potatoes

INGREDIENTS:
8 cups water or low sodium vegetable broth
2 Tablespoons sun-dried tomato powder
2 leeks (approximately 6 ounces), thinly sliced
2-3 large sweet potatoes (2 pounds), peeled and cut into uniform cubes
2 cans cannellini beans, rinsed and drained
1 pound rainbow chard, chopped
1/4 cup fresh squeezed lemon juice (with zest from lemons)

METHOD:
In a large soup pot, bring the water or vegetable broth to a boil. Reduce heat to medium and add the leeks. Cook for about 8 minutes until soft. Add diced sweet potatoes and cook another 8-10 minutes until tender. Add the beans and cook for an additional 2 minutes. Remove soup pot from heat and stir in chard so that it wilts. Stir in lemon juice and sun-dried tomato powder. Sprinkle chopped Italian parsley on top, if desired, and garnish with a fresh lemon twist. The preparation for this soup can be done in advance. You can have the leeks sliced, the sweet potatoes diced, the beans rinsed, the chard chopped, the juice squeezed and the water measured out. Then it takes only 20 minutes to cook it. This recipe can easily be doubled.

Chef's Note: With the bright orange sweet potatoes, white beans, and rainbow colored chard, this is a very pretty soup. But if you can't find rainbow chard, feel free to substitute Swiss chard or any greens such as collards, spinach or kale.

TOMATO AND TORTILLA SOUP

INGREDIENTS:
4 cups red onion, finely diced (about 3)
6 cloves garlic, minced or put through a garlic press
4 x 14.5 ounce cans salt-free diced tomatoes
4 cups water
2 Tablespoons sundried tomato powder
1 teaspoon chili powder
12 small corn tortillas (oil and salt free), cut into sixths (one 12-ounce package)
1/4 cups fresh lime juice (approximately 2)
Avocado and cilantro, for garnish, if desired

METHOD:
Water sauté the onions for 8-10 minutes until soft and translucent. Add the garlic and cook for another 2-3 minutes. Add the tomatoes and water and bring to a boil. Stir in the sundried tomato powder until dissolved and add the chili powder. Reduce heat, add the tortillas, cover and simmer for 12-15 minutes until the tortillas are soft and broken down. Remove from heat and stir in lime juice. Garnish with sliced avocado and cilantro, if desired.

Chef's Note: Normally, to thicken a soup, you use a roux made from butter, flour and cream. The corn tortillas do the same thing as they break down, giving the soup a creamy texture and mouth feel but in a more healthful way.

SENSATIONAL SIDES

5 MINUTE CRANBERRY RELISH

(Raw)

Why cook your relish or use sugar when you can make this instead?

INGREDIENTS:
1 x 12 ounce bag fresh cranberries
2 large peeled oranges (zest included)
Dates, to taste
2 Tablespoons psyllium husk

METHOD:
In a food processor fitted with the "S" blade, process all of the ingredients until the desired chunky texture is reached. Adding fresh ginger and lime juice is also a delicious variation.

Chef's Note: This is also delicious on your morning oatmeal.

EASY, CHEESY, PEASIES
(Raw)

INGREDIENTS:
1 pound frozen peas, defrosted
1 cup raw cashews, soaked
1/4 cup nutritional yeast
1/4 cup low sodium miso paste
1/4 cup fresh lemon juice
1/4 cup water
4 cloves garlic (more or less, to taste)
1/4 teaspoon red pepper flakes
1/2 teaspoon turmeric

METHOD:
Drain and rinse cashews. Place all ingredients (except for peas) in a food processor fitted with the "S" blade and process until smooth. Pour over peas and mix well. Chill well before serving.

FAUX PARMESAN

(Raw)

This is much more economical than the store-bought version.

INGREDIENTS:
1 cup raw almonds or cashews
1/2 cup nutritional yeast
1 Tablespoon salt-free seasoning (I prefer Benson's Table Tasty.)

METHOD:
In a food processor fitted with the "S" blade or in a blender, combine all ingredients until a powdery texture is achieved. If you like it more chunky, process less.

Chef's Note: You can also use store-bought almond flour in place of the almonds. We use this on everything from air popped popcorn to potatoes to steamed veggies and as a topping on chili and soups.

FRUITY QUINOA

A great change of pace from your morning oatmeal.

INGREDIENTS:
1/2 cup quinoa
1 cup orange juice
1/2 teaspoon cinnamon
1 teaspoon alcohol-free vanilla
2 Tablespoons currants or unsweetened dried cranberries

METHOD:
Place quinoa, orange juice, cinnamon and vanilla in a sauce pan and bring to a boil. Reduce to a simmer, cover, and cook 10-15 minutes, until all of the liquid is absorbed. Stir in dried fruit.

HOLIDAY BAKED YAMS

If I had a nickel for every time someone asked me the difference between a yam and a sweet potato, I could retire. They're both delicious (and I still don't know)!

INGREDIENTS:
4 large yams, peeled and diced
2 ripe pears, peeled and diced
1 cup unsweetened dried cranberries
1/2 cup fresh orange juice
1 Tablespoon alcohol-free vanilla

METHOD:
Preheat oven to 350 degrees F. Mix all ingredients together and place in a baking dish that has a lid. Cover and bake for one hour (or until soft). You should easily be able to pierce the yams with a fork.

MAPLE GLAZED BRUSSELS SPROUTS

Even people who say they don't normally like Brussels sprouts will enjoy this dish.

INGREDIENTS:
1 and 1/2 pound Brussels sprouts
1/4 cup finely minced shallot
1/4 cup maple syrup
1Tablespoon Dijon mustard
1 Tablespoon low sodium tamari
1 Tablespoon arrowroot powder
Finely diced red bell pepper (optional)
Chopped candied walnuts or spiced pecans (optional)

METHOD:
Cut off stems from Brussels sprouts and then cut in half. Cook for 2 minutes in boiling water. Drain and rinse in cold water. (This step can be done in advance.) In a heavy nonstick sauce pan, sauté shallots in vegetable broth or water for 2-3 minutes. Add Brussels sprouts and sauté for 4 minutes longer. Whisk together maple syrup, tamari, Dijon mustard and arrowroot. Pour over vegetables and cook 2 minutes longer until sauce is thickened. Garnish with red bell pepper or nuts, if desired.

Chef's Note: If you don't want to use maple syrup, use date syrup and add 1/4 to 1/2 teaspoon of maple extract.

MASHED NOtatoes

If you serve this with gravy,
no one would know these aren't potatoes.

INGREDIENTS:
1 head of cauliflower
Nutritional yeast or Faux Parmesan (page 142), to taste

METHOD:
Steam or blanch cauliflower until soft. Place cauliflower in a food processer fitted with the "S" blade and process until smooth and creamy. Add seasonings to taste and process again.

Chef's Note: Don't be surprised if you end up eating the whole head all by yourself! You can also do this with parsnips.

MISO COLLARDS WITH A KICK

Thank you Jetta Mason for sharing this recipe.

INGREDIENTS:
2 bunches collard greens (cut stem out like a V and chop leaves into medium pieces)
1/2 large brown onion, sliced thin
1-2 Tablespoons diced Mezzetta jalapenos (optional)
3 cloves fresh garlic, diced fine or pressed
1 cup carrots, sliced thin
2 Tablespoons low sodium miso paste, dissolved in 3/4 cup water
Drizzle of low sodium tamari (optional)

METHOD:
Over medium heat, water sauté garlic, onions and jalapenos until onions are translucent. Add carrots and sauté another few minutes. Add miso and water mixture and allow to thicken slightly, stirring frequently. Once miso thickens, place collard leafs on top, cover, and turn down heat. You can drizzle a little soy sauce on top of collards before covering. When leaves start to wilt, stir everything together. Cook for another 5-10 minutes.

OVEN ROASTED CARAMELIZED ONIONS

Thank you Zel Allen, author of "The Nut Gourmet", for allowing me to share this ingenious recipe. Zel's website is www.vegparadise.com and her blog is http://nutgourmet.wordpress.com.

INGREDIENTS:
3 medium onions, sliced about 3/8 inch thick
1 teaspoon balsamic vinegar
1 teaspoon low sodium tamari

METHOD:
Preheat oven to 375 degrees. Double stack the onions into the center of a jellyroll pan and roast them for 15 minutes. Using a spatula, turn the onions over, piling them into the center of the pan. Roast 15 minutes longer. Turn the onions again and separate them into a single layer. Roast 10 minutes longer. Add the balsamic vinegar and soy sauce and use the spatula to mix well. Spread the onions into a single layer and roast 10 minutes longer.

PICO DE GALLO
(Raw)

INGREDIENTS:
3 firm Roma tomatoes
1 jalapeño pepper
1 shallot
2 cloves garlic
1 lime
Chopped cilantro, to taste

METHOD:
Cut tomatoes in half, squeeze out extra juice and seeds, and then dice. Place in a bowl and add the lime juice. Dice the shallots and garlic and add to the tomatoes. Finely dice the jalapeño, removing the seeds if you would like it less hot. Add to the tomatoes. Season with chopped cilantro and stir.

Chef's Note: Sometimes, I will add a finely diced red bell pepper.

PINEAPPLE UNFRIED RICE

A great way to use leftover brown rice

INGREDIENTS:
1 large can crushed unsweetened pineapple, drained
(save the juice for sautéing without oil)
1 cup green peas
1 bunch scallions
1 red bell pepper, diced fine
4 ounces pea pods, sliced
1 bunch cilantro leaves, chopped
4 cups cooked brown rice, chilled
1/2 cup low sodium tamari

METHOD:
Heat 1/2 cup of the pineapple juice in a wok or non-stick skillet over medium-high heat. Add peppers and scallions and sauté 2-3 minutes. Add peas, pea pods and rice and cook for another 2-3 minutes. Add pineapple and tamari and cook for another minute or so. If mixture becomes too dry, add more pineapple juice as you are sautéing. Remove from heat, stir in cilantro, and serve.

Chef's Note: For a spectacular presentation, serve in a hollowed out fresh pineapple half.

QUINOA SALAD WITH CURRANTS AND PISTACHIOS

Try red quinoa for a colorful change of pace.

INGREDIENTS:
1-16 ounce box of quinoa, cooked and cooled
1 cup lime juice and zest from limes (approximately 8)
1 ounce finely chopped scallions
1/2 ounce finely chopped Italian parsley
1/2 ounce finely chopped mint
2 cups currants
8 ounces raw pistachios

METHOD:
Prepare quinoa according to the directions on the package. Place in large bowl and allow to cool. Juice and zest limes. Pour over quinoa. Add remaining ingredients and mix well. Chill.

Chef's Note: Add pomegranate seeds when in season. Try substituting orange juice and zest for the lime, or unsweetened cherries for the currants.

SAUCY GLAZED MUSHROOMS

INGREDIENTS:
1 red onion, finely diced
2 pounds sliced mushrooms
4 cloves garlic, pressed (or more to taste)
Low-sodium tamari

METHOD:
Pour tamari over garlic and mushrooms and let marinate several hours or overnight. Drain mushrooms, reserving liquid. Sauté onion in the leftover tamari in a non-stick pan until nicely browned, approximately 10 minutes, adding more tamari, a tablespoon at a time, if pan becomes dry. Add drained mushrooms and sauté until all the liquid is absorbed and mushrooms have a nice glaze over them.

Chef's Note: This is also delicious over pasta.

SPANISH "RICE"

(Raw)

By grating the cauliflower, it resembles rice.

INGREDIENTS:
1 head of orange cauliflower
4 green onions, diced
2 tomatoes, diced
1 orange bell pepper, diced
2 Tablespoons fresh lemon juice
1/2 cup chopped cilantro
2 avocados, mashed
1 Tablespoon paprika
1 teaspoon chili powder
1 jalapeño pepper, diced (optional)

METHOD:
In a food processor fitted with the grating blade, grate the cauliflower. Mix in the remainder of the ingredients by hand.

Chef's Note: If you can't find an orange cauliflower, a white one is fine. If you want your dish less spicy, omit the seeds from the jalapeño. Make sure you wear gloves when cutting hot peppers and never touch your eyes!

SPICY PEANUT NOODLES WITH BROCCOLI

This reminds me of the peanut noodles from Chin Chin.

INGREDIENTS:
1 pound brown rice noodles (spaghetti or linguine)
1 pound broccoli florets
3/4 cup peanut butter, unsweetened and unsalted
3/4 cup water
1/4 cup rice vinegar
2 Tablespoons low sodium tamari
2 Tablespoons date syrup
2 cloves garlic, pressed
1/4 - 1/2 ounce piece fresh ginger, pressed
1/2 teaspoon red pepper flakes
8 scallions, thinly sliced on the diagonal
Sesame seeds or chopped unsalted peanuts for garnish (optional)

METHOD:
Cook pasta according to directions on package. Run under cold water when done. Drain and place in a large bowl. Blanch broccoli and run under cold water when done. Drain and add to pasta bowl along with the scallions. To make the sauce, combine peanut butter, water, rice vinegar, tamari, date syrup, garlic, ginger and red pepper in a saucepan over medium-high heat. Whisk until smooth and cook for about 10 minutes until thickened. Pour dressing over noodles and broccoli and thoroughly combine. Chill until it becomes cold.

TWICE BAKED STUFFED SWEET POTATOES

This is so pretty and tastes as good as it looks.
It's a great way to use your leftover cranberry relish.

INGREDIENTS:
4 - 5 medium sweet potatoes
1/2 cup Cranberry Relish (page 140)
1/2 cup dried unsweetened cranberries
1/2 cups pecans (optional)

METHOD:
Bake sweet potatoes until tender. Cool slightly and then cut in half. Scoop pulp from each potato half leaving about a 1/4" border so that the potato half will stand up and can be filled. Mash sweet potatoes with a potato masher and add cranberry relish and dried cranberries. Mix well to combine. Scoop potato mixture evenly into potato shells. Sprinkle with pecans, if desired. Bake in a 350 degree F preheated oven for 30 minutes or until heated through.

TRUFFLES

In the middle of the *30 Day Unprocessed Challenge*, we have a "Ball-Off." The participants create their own truffles made of any combination of fruit, nuts and seeds, and their creations are judged by a panel of celebrity judges. Here are some of the winning recipes, along with a few of my own.

ALMOND DREAM BALLS

(Raw)

Nataly Carranza won first place with this recipe.

INGREDIENTS:
1/2 cup raw almonds
1/4 cup raw walnuts
1/2 cup pitted dates
1/4 cup raw almond butter
1/2 teaspoon almond extract
shredded coconut

METHOD:
Place the almonds and walnuts into the food processor and process until coarsely chopped. Add the dates, almond butter, and almond extract and process until the mixture holds together. Place the shredded coconut into a small bowl. Remove 1 Tablespoon of the date/nut mixture from the processor at a time and roll into 1-inch balls. Roll the balls in the shredded coconut to coat completely.

ALMOND OVERJOY BALLS

(Raw)

Kitchen Angel, Brenda Cohen, came in a close second with these.

INGREDIENTS:
2 cups raw almonds
1/4 cup raw cacao powder
2 cups pitted deglet noor dates
1/4 cup raw shredded coconut (macaroon cut)
1/2 cup golden raisins
1 Tablespoon alcohol-free vanilla extract
1/4 teaspoon almond extract (or to taste)
Equal parts cacao and shredded coconut for rolling

METHOD:
In a food processor fitted with the "S" blade, process the almonds until they are almost nut-butter consistency. Add cacao powder and process again until fully incorporated. Add dates and process again until mixture almost comes together. Add coconut and process again until thoroughly combined. Add raisins and extracts until the mixture will stick together and form a ball if rolled (clumped) in your hand. Roll into balls, and then roll in cacao and coconut mixture. Enjoy!

APPLE PIE HEARTS
(Raw)

INGREDIENTS:
1 cup almonds
1 cup pecans
1 cup walnuts
2 cups dried apples (sugar and sulfite free)
2 cups pitted dates
1 Tablespoon alcohol-free vanilla extract
1 Tablespoon cinnamon
1/4 - 1/2 teaspoon nutmeg

METHOD:
In a food processor fitted with the "S" blade, grind nuts into flour. Add the dried apple and spices and process again. Add the dates until the desired consistency is reached, then add the vanilla. Press into mini silicon heart molds and chill.

Chef's Note: If you don't have silicone molds, just roll them into balls.

bRAWnies
(Raw)

INGREDIENTS:
2 cups walnuts
2 cups pitted dates
1/2 cup raw cacao powder or carob powder
1 Tablespoon alcohol-free vanilla extract

METHOD:
In a food processor fitted with the "S" blade, process walnuts into a powder. Do not over process into a nut butter. Add the cacao or carob powder and process again. Add the dates until a ball forms. Then add the vanilla and briefly process again. Place into a silicone brownie mold or in an 8" x 8" square pan and freeze until firm.

Chef's Note: You can use any raw nut or seed (or combination) instead of the walnuts.

CHOCOLATE CHIP CHERRY BITES
(Raw)

INGREDIENTS:
2 cups raw pecans
1/2 cup raw cacao powder
8 ounces dried cherries (unsweetened and unsulfured)
8 ounces pitted dates
1/4 cup raw cacao nibs
1 Tablespoon alcohol-free vanilla extract
1/4 teaspoon cherry extract

METHOD:
In a food processor fitted with the "S" blade, process the nuts into a flour. Add the cacao powder and process again briefly. Add the cherries and process again, then the dates. If mixture is not sticky enough to reach the "break point", add more dates or a splash of date syrup. Then add the extracts and process again briefly, then the nibs and pulse. Press mixture into a silicone brownie pan.

CHOCOLATE HAZELNUT GIANDUIA TRUFFLES

(Pronunciation: zhahn-DOO-yuh.)
Recipe by Michelle Wolf.
Consulting Taster: Husband, Alan Raz.

INGREDIENTS:
1-1/2 cups raw hazelnut (divided)
18 deglet noor pitted dates (soaked overnight in unsweetened chocolate almond milk)
2 Tablespoons Ultimate brand raw cacao powder (for dark chocolate flavor)
Alcohol-free vanilla extract (optional)
Alcohol-free almond extract (optional)

METHOD:
Place 1/2 cup of hazelnuts into the food processor and process until ground into a coarse powder. Place into a bowl and set aside. (To be used later to coat the outside of the truffles.) Place remaining 1 cup of hazelnuts into the food processor and process until ground into a coarse powder. Add cacao powder and the soaked dates (without excess soaking liquid). To enhance the subtle flavor blend, you can try adding 1/2-1 teaspoon of vanilla extract and 1/4 teaspoon of almond extract. Process until the mixture becomes a thick paste. Remove by rounded teaspoon and place a whole hazelnut into the center of the chocolate nut mixture. Roll in palm of hands to form small round balls, approximately 1" in diameter. To avoid sticking, slightly wet palms of hands before rolling each ball. Roll each ball in bowl of ground hazelnuts until outside is even coated. Place into container and store in freezer until ready to serve.

FIGGY FLAX

(Raw)

Thank you Robin Fomalont for this easy, tasty recipe.

INGREDIENTS:
1/2 cup dates
1/2 cup figs
1 cup raw cashews
Toasted flax seeds (for rolling)

METHOD:
Blend dates, figs, and cashews in a food processor. Form into balls, and roll the balls in toasted flax seeds.

Chef's Note: You can always use dried figs in place of dates in just about any recipe.

GOJI BERRY TRUFFLES

(Raw)

These little gems are more mostly fruit and contain no nuts.

INGREDIENTS:
1/2 cup hemp seeds
1/2 cup pumpkin seeds
1 cup goji berries
1/2 cup dark raisins
1 and 1/2 cups pitted dates
1/2 cup raw cacao powder or carob powder
1 Tablespoon alcohol-free vanilla extract

METHOD:
In a food processor fitted with the "S" blade, process seeds into a powder. Add goji berries and process again. Then add raisins and dates and process again until mixture begins to stick together. Add vanilla and process again briefly. Place in a silicone mold or form into balls.

HELLUVA HALVAH BITTY BALL

(Raw)

Another delicious recipe from Brenda Cohen, who makes all of my recipes better than I do!

INGREDIENTS:
1/2 cup raw sesame seeds
2 teaspoon raw cacao or carob powder
1/2 teaspoon maca powder
Dash of cinnamon
2 Tablespoons yacon syrup (could use date syrup)
1 Tablespoon raw tahini
1 teaspoon vanilla extract
1 Tablespoon raw cacao nibs

METHOD:
Add ingredients to a food processor one at a time until a cohesive mass forms. Roll into bitty balls and enjoy!

LUSCIOUS LEMON CHOCOLATE COATED TRUFFLE

Kitchen Angel Michelle Wolf brought this over the night the Esselstyns came for dinner and was quite honored when Ann Esselstyn, a wonderful cook and cookbook author, asked for the recipe.

Note: Allow time to soak dates overnight for both the Lemon Center and the Chocolate Coating.

INGREDIENTS: (Lemon Center)
1/2 cup raw almonds
1/2 cup raw cashews
18 deglet noor pitted dates
Lemon zest
Lemon juice
Unsweetened almond milk
1/2 teaspoon lemon extract

METHOD: (Lemon Center)
Soak dates overnight in mixture of 2/3 lemon juice and 1/3 unsweetened almond milk. Place 1/2 cup of almonds and 1/2 cup of raw cashews into the food processor and process until ground into coarse powder. Add soaked dates, a few at a time, to monitor texture of lemon filling. Add zest from squeezed lemon. Add 1/2 teaspoon of lemon extract to bump up lemon flavor. Remove by rounded 1/2 teaspoonfuls. Roll in palm of hands to form small round balls approximately 3/4" in diameter. (To avoid sticking, slightly wet palms of hands before rolling each ball.) Place into container so that balls are not touching. Close container and place into freezer until balls become frozen solid.

INGREDIENTS: (Chocolate Coating)
1 cup raw hazelnuts or pecans
3/4 cup raw almonds
3/4 cup hazelnuts
18 deglet noor pitted dates (soaked overnight in unsweetened chocolate almond milk)
3 Tablespoons Ultimate brand raw cacao powder (for dark chocolate flavor)
Alcohol-free vanilla extract (optional)
Alcohol-free almond extract (optional)

METHOD: (Chocolate Coating)
Place 1 cup of hazelnuts or pecans into the food processor and process until ground into a fine powder. Place into a bowl and set aside. (To be used later to coat the outside of the truffles.) Place 3/4 cup of almonds and 3/4 cup of hazelnuts into the food processor and process until ground into coarse powder. Add cacao powder and the soaked dates (without excess soaking liquid). To enhance the subtle flavor blend, you can try adding 1/2 - 1 teaspoon of vanilla extract and 1/4 teaspoon of almond extract. Process until the mixture becomes a thick paste. Now, remove lemon balls from the freezer. Scoop from chocolate mixture by rounded teaspoon-full and flatten between thumbs and first fingers. Place lemon ball in the center and wrap chocolate coating entirely around center filling. When completely encased, roll in palm of hands to form round balls approximately 1-1/4" in diameter. (To avoid sticking, slightly wet palms of hands before rolling each ball.) Roll each ball in bowl of ground hazelnuts (or pecans) until outside is evenly coated. Place into container and store in freezer until ready to serve.

PB & J BITES

These taste like my favorite Lara Bar flavor,
but without the added salt.

INGREDIENTS:
2 cups unsalted peanuts
1 cup pitted dates
1 cup unsweetened dried cherries
1 Tablespoon alcohol-free vanilla

METHOD:
In a food processor fitted with the "S" blade, process peanuts into a powder. Add dates and cherries and process until a ball forms. Add vanilla and process again briefly. Roll into balls or place in a silicone brownie mold pan.

PEANUT BITES

INGREDIENTS:
2 cups of unsalted, roasted peanuts (or other raw nut)
2 cups of pitted dates
1 Tablespoon alcohol-free vanilla extract

METHOD:
In a food processor fitted with the "S" blade, process the nuts until they are a flour-like consistency. Do not over process or you will have a nut butter. Add dates, a few at a time, until the mixture clumps together. Stop the machine and if you can easily roll a ball from the mixture and it sticks together, you don't need to add any more dates. Roll into balls. You can also roll the balls in coconut, crushed nuts or raw carob or cacao powder.

Chef's Note: Delicious when you mix in some raw cacao nibs. If you have a dehydrator, you can roll the batter into a ball, press it flat into a circle, and then dehydrate. It tastes just like a peanut butter cookie!

PEANUT BUTTER FUDGE TRUFFLES

Two great tastes that taste great together

INGREDIENTS:
1 batch of Chocolate FUNdue (page 64)
Chopped unsalted peanuts

METHOD:
Prepare FUNdue and place in glass bowl and chill until firm. Using a small cookie scoop, measure out the FUNdue and roll in chopped peanuts. Freeze until firm.

Chef's Notes: I like to put these on individual candy papers. I buy *See's Candies* boxes and put them inside and fool people all the time! You can make a raw version of these treats by using raw almond butter, raw cashew butter or tahini.

TROPICAL TREATS

(Raw)

Yi Fan Rao won the very first Ball-off with this tasty treat.

INGREDIENTS:
1 1/2 cups raw almonds
1 cup macadamia nuts, roughly chopped
1 cup dried pineapple, diced
1 cup dried apricots, diced
1/2 cup raw almonds, roughly chopped
10 to 12 dates, soaked in water overnight
1 cup golden flax seeds

METHOD:
Grind the raw almonds into a fine meal in the food processor and transfer to a large bowl. Add the macadamias, pineapple, apricots and the 1/2 cup chopped almonds to the bowl. Chop the dates and add them to the bowl. Mix well until the mixture becomes sticky. Form the mixture into 1-inch balls by rolling between the palms of the hands, then, roll the balls in the flax seeds to coat them completely. Place the balls into a covered container and freeze. Serve the balls frozen, partly defrosted, or room temperature.

Chef's Note: You could also roll them in sesame seeds.

RESOURCES

These are a few of my favorite things.

Recommended Reading

Breaking the Food Seduction by Neal Barnard, M.D.
Building Bone Vitality by Amy Joy Lanou, Ph.D. and Michael Castleman
Change or Die by Alan Deutschman
The Complete Idiot's Guide to Plant-Based Nutrition by Julieanna Hever, M.S., R.D., C.P.T.
Eat To Live by Joel Fuhrman, M.D.
The China Study by T. Colin Campbell, Ph.D.
The End of Overeating by David Kessler, M.D.
The Engine 2 Diet by Rip Esselstyn
Feelings Buried Alive Never Die by Karol Truman
The Health Promoting Cookbook by Alan Goldhamer, D.C.
Keep It Simple, Keep it Whole by Matthew Lederman, M.D. and Alona Pulde, M.D.
Mad Cowboy by Howard Lyman with Glen Merzer
The McDougall Plan by John McDougall, M.D.
Mindless Eating by Brian Wansink
No More Bull! by Howard Lyman with Glen Merzer and Joanna Samorow-Merzer
Prevent and Reverse Heart Disease by Caldwell B. Esselstyn, Jr., M.D.
The Pleasure Trap by Doug Lisle, Ph.D. & Alan Goldhamer, D.C.
When Food is Love by Geneen Roth
You Can Heal Your Life by Louise Hay
1,000 Vegan Recipes by Robin Robertson (Just leave out the sugar, oil and salt.)

DVDs

Chef AJ's Holiday Recipes
Fast Food by Jeff Novick (www.jeffnovick.com)
Forks Over Knives
Healthy Made Delicious (Chef AJ and Dr. Matt)
Processed People by Jeff & Sabrina Nelson (www.processedpeople.com)
To Your Health by Julieanna Hever and Jesse Pomeroy

Healing Centers

www.drmcdougall.com
www.healthpromoting.com
www.optimumhealth.org

Raw Restaurants

www.aulac.com
www.cafegratitude.com
www.crusilverlake.com
www.maryssecretgarden.net
www.rawsheeds.com

Vegan Restaurants

www.millenniumrestaurant.com
www.nativefoods.com
www.realfood.com
www.seedkitchen.com
www.sublimerestaurant.com
www.veggiegrill.com

Vegan Friendly Restaurants

www.sojournercafe.com
www.followyourheart.com
www.grassrootsnaturalmarket.net
www.hugosrestaurant.com
www.mcafedechaya.com
www.pizzacookery.com
www.spiritlandbistro.com

Websites

www.ChefAJsHealthyKitchen.com
www.chipusa.org
www.drfuhrman.com
www.drmcdougall.com
www.fatfreevegan.com
www.happycow.net
www.happyherbivore.com
www.HealthyTasteofLA.com
www.heartattackproof.com
www.pcrm.org
www.plantbaseddietitian.com
www.vegparadise.com
www.vegsource.com
www.wellnessforum.com

Quotes

"How did we get to a place where the companies who profit from our sickness are the ones telling us how to be healthy; how the companies that profit from our food choices are the ones telling us what to eat?"
T. Colin Campbell, Ph.D.

"I don't understand why asking people to eat a well-balanced vegetarian diet is considered drastic, while it is medically conservative to cut people open and put them on cholesterol lowering drugs for the rest of their lives."
Dean Ornish, M.D.

"America is a constipated nation.... If you pass small stools, you have to have large hospitals."
Denis Burkitt

"Diseases can rarely be eliminated through early diagnosis or good treatment, but prevention can eliminate disease. "
Denis Burkitt

"If people are constantly falling off a cliff, you could place ambulances under the cliff or build a fence on the top of the cliff. We are placing all too many ambulances under the cliff."
Denis Burkitt

"The animals of the world exist for their own reasons. They were not made for humans any more than black people were made for white, or women created for men."
Alice Walker

"If God made it, eat it. If man made it, don't eat it."
Jack LaLanne

INDEX

CPSIA information can be obtained
at www.ICGtesting.com
Printed in the USA
BVOW06s1913201117
500932BV00012B/359/P